edition Wissensc

Raphael D. Thöne

Malcolm Arnold - A Composer of Real Music
Symphonic Writing, Style and Aesthetics

Raphael D. Thöne
Malcolm Arnold - A Composer of Real Music
Symphonic Writing, Style and Aesthetics

© edition Wissenschaft

First published 2007.
Copyright © 2007 by Raphael D. Thöne
Copy-Editing: Deborah Hodgson
Cover Portrait: Gerhard van der Grinten Esq.
Printed and bound in the UK by
Lightning Source UK Ltd, Milton Keynes
Printed and bound in the US by
Lightning Source Inc (US), La Vergne
ISBN 3-937748-06-7
ISBN 978-3-937748-06-1

German National Library Cataloguing-in-Publication Data:
A catalogue record for this book is available from the
German National Library.
see http://dnb.d-nb.de

Edition Wissenschaft is an academic Publishing division of
Entercom Saurus Records KG.

Contents

0.1 List of Figures

0.2 Preface and Acknowledgments

I still remember the day when I first heard one of Malcolm Arnold's orchestral works on a childhood visit to my uncle Michael's place in London.

While Michael dealt with his annual 'good fortune' of hosting our family, we were for our part thrilled by the chance to explore the various nooks and crannies of the great city in which he lived and worked. From noisy Shepherds Bush to Notting Hill Gate, Richmond, Bayswater, even the Docklands East London, we would wander around. In 1994, when I was 14, we found ourselves attending the *Music on a Summer Evening* festival, organised by English Heritage and set in four beautiful, charming gardens. That 2 July took us to Kenwood, where the Wren Symphony Orchestra, under the direction of Hilary Davan Wetton, was playing a series of pieces created exclusively by British composers. Alongside a premier by Howard Blake, we heard Holst's *Planets*, Elgar's *Cockaigne* overture, Delius' *Walk to the Paradise Garden* and Arnold's *Cornish Dances*, Opus 91.

By that time, I had already begun composing and was thrilled by this impressive display of British music that was so different from the European-continental avant-garde style to which I had been accustomed. When I later found myself tackling Arnold's main symphonic works as a composition student, I would look back to that special evening and wonder whether fate had been looking down upon me then. I must have spent hours searching through my room just to find that yellowing old programme.

I would like to take this moment to thank those who have supported and guided me in my study of Arnold's symphonic work. Above all, I should mention my two supervisors, Prof Dieter Torkewitz (University of Music and Performing Arts in Vienna) and Prof Manfred Angerer (University of Vienna), who have both skilfully guided me through my work and whose critical yet candid comments provided invaluable assistance. I would like to particularly thank Prof Torkewitz for encouraging me to take a stance on Arnold and not shy away from forming my own ideas. He also made the extremely helpful suggestion that I highlight and analyse the crossover effect in Arnold's composition. At the same time, I am also very grateful to Prof Angerer for introducing me to Terry Eagleton, whose writings sharpened my observation skills and cast light on the British point of view.

This work in its present form would not have been possible without the support of Anthony Day and Fiona Southey. Anthony not only arranged for me to meet Sir Malcolm Arnold in Attleborough in February 2006, but also consistently and patiently listened to my thoughts and provided much enlightenment through his stories about his life with Sir Malcolm. He always made me feel at home with his predilection for Nescafé and his ability to constantly pull my leg with his British sense of humour. Fiona, meanwhile, is quite simply a gorgeous person. I have rarely met such a truly open, likeable and all-the-while professional promotion manager. She anticipated my every request, even enabling me to gain direct access to Arnold's sketches. Thanks to you both for your support.

I would also like to thank Sir Malcolm's daughter, Katherine Arnold, for her eagerness to help. The same goes for my many colleagues and fellow PhD students in Vienna, with whom I was able to exchange my personal views on Malcolm Arnold. The special atmosphere in Vienna definitely had a very positive influence on my thinking. Special contributions came from Helena Langewitz (the lady with the wonderful voice), Dainis Michel (look at it another way...), Martin Kappeler (precision and knowledge in one) and Ksenija (Nina) Zadravec (Sushi at Landstraße). The meeting with Dr Karl (Horand) Tekusch was of particularly great benefit. Horand shared his knowledge and ideas with me and did not, as he frequently mentioned, bombard me with suggestions. Instead, he took me very seriously. Of my friends in Germany, I should also mention Gabriella Sinay (Arnold's flute sonata never sounded better) and Carolin Surowetz.

I am further grateful to the 'good souls' at Moers central library, Ms Gummersbach and Mr Richter, for their ability to obtain every book requested. I would also like to thank Dr Peter Horton from the reference library at the Royal College of Music in London who made every article available for my visits and, most importantly, opened up all of Arnold's original manuscripts. Here I should also thank the Arnold Estate for granting permission to print his sketches.

I appreciate the assistance of Boosey and Hawkes Ltd (Mike Wood), Faber Music Ltd (Sheree Bevins), Ricordi Ltd (Miranda Jackson) and Novello and Co Ltd (James Rushton and Caroyln Fuller) in allowing the reproduction of the scores.

Gerhard van der Grinten Esq. and Günther Kögebehn were able to give me much encouragement during the inaugural Arnold Festival 2006 in Northampton. Gerhard, with whom I have been friends for many years, opened Arnold's work up to me in a very special way. I am indebted to him for his portrait – it is truly fascinating.

I would also like to express my appreciation for the legendary Arnold concert at Moyland Castle on the lower Rhine, which was a huge success and united us in our appreciation of Arnold's music.

Meeting Piers Burton-Page and Paul Harris, the authors of Arnold's previous biographies, and discussing Arnold with them face-to-face also brought about valuable new insights.

Thanks also go to my uncle Michael who put me up during my 'fieldwork' in London and prevented me from being devoured by 'their Canine Highness'.

I would also like to thank Deborah (Debi) Hodgson for her English copy-editing – her linguistic and personal sensitivity to my ideas was invaluable for my work.

Finally, I dedicate this book to my parents Angelika and Hans-Georg, my brother Björn Philippe and sister Leonie Viola, who have always been willing to lend me an ear.

Vienna, June 2007

0.2 Preface and Acknowledgments

1. Methodology and Topic

The premises imposed by Umberto Eco on choosing a topic and his specific requirements for the scientific method within a paper do not pose a corset-like constraint on any research paper within the humanities. Rather, they legitimise the reason that an initial personal affinity toward a certain topic, an academic interest in a subject, a whim or, in the case of music, a specific musical work and its composer turns into the subject of scientific research (ECO 2005:16 et seqq.). Eco's four core assumptions seemingly only repeat what has already been established or said, and their conciseness represents the level at which the author wishes to approach the symphonic works of Malcolm Arnold:

„...1. Die Untersuchung behandelt einen erkennbaren Gegenstand, der so genau umrissen ist, dass er auch für Dritte erkennbar ist... (...*The piece of research deals with an identifiable subject outlined in such a way that it is identifiable by third parties...)[1]*

2. Die Untersuchung muss über diesen Gegenstand Dinge sagen, die noch nicht gesagt worden sind, oder sie muss Dinge, die schon gesagt worden sind, aus einem neuen Blickwinkel sehen... (*The piece of research must say something about this subject that has not already been said or must look at it from a different angle...)*

3. Die Untersuchung muss für andere von Nutzen sein... Eine Arbeit ist wissenschaftlich, wenn sie (bei Beachtung der Regeln 1 und 2) dem etwas hinzufügt, was bisher der wissenschaftlichen Öffentlichkeit bekannt war und wenn alle künftigen Arbeiten zum gleichen Thema ihre Ergebnisse, zumindest theoretisch, berücksichtigen müssen...

(The piece of research must be of use to other people...A paper is scientific if it (under consideration of rules 1 and 2) adds something to what is already known to the scientific community and if all future works on the same topic must consider its results, at least theoretically ...)

4. Die Untersuchung muss jene Angaben enthalten, die ermöglichen nachzuprüfen, ob ihre Hypothesen falsch oder richtig sind...Das ist eine fundamentale Anforderung... (*The piece of research must contain information enabling one to verify whether its assumptions are right or wrong. This is a fundamental requirement...)* (ECO 2005:40-45):

I will briefly explain these four requirements as they pertain to the British composer Malcolm Arnold (1921 [Northampton]–2006 [Norfolk]).

---

[1] If a standard English translation is available, I have quoted from it. In several cases, I have translated the original German text to English. However, I have always included the original German quotation from which conclusions have been drawn.

Arnold's oeuvre[2] contains stage works, works for symphonic orchestra, instrumental concertos, and works for chamber music ensembles – from solo to larger instrumental ensembles such as string orchestras, but also woodwinds quintets as well as various brass ensembles (brass dectets, English brass bands) – and to a lesser extent compositions for accompanied voice or choir.

However, this creative compositional work is enriched by a huge amount of film music that should not be viewed separately from the concertante oeuvre. The simplified distinction made in German-speaking areas between so-called "serious" music and "light" music (film music, also termed "functional" music, is generally assigned to the latter) all too often reflects an aesthetic devaluation.[3] One could disregard analytical issues about the structure, syntax, and form, or, in short, the compositional fracture, due to the fact that film music is seen as merely a servant of the picture.

In the case of Arnold, a strict separation of concertante and film work would ignore the fact that these musical worlds are mutually dependent. Arnold's symphonies cannot be explained without considering his film-music writing techniques, and his advanced programmatic tone poems, which use a tonal language of fragility and atonality, are clearly influenced by the symphonic writing of his concercante music.

Again, the identifiable subject of this dissertation is Arnold's symphonic orchestral music and categorising it in the context of British contemporary music of the twentieth century. This selection covers a) aspects of historical development (the development of Arnold's personal style), b) relevance to research (attempts to describe Arnold's composition processes on the basis of case studies of sketches – instrumentation particells like piano short scores – and full scores), and c) personal preference and subjective evaluation (the meaning and interpretation of the work).

The image of Arnold created by the author through his own selection of symphonic works for analysis will understandably be different from that created by Burton-Page (1994), Cole (1989), Harris/Meredith (2004), or Jackson (2003), and will critically question these earlier analyses.[4]

---

[2] The following directories of works mentioned here are the most thorough: Craggs (CRAGGS 1989:9-118), Harris/Meredith (HARRIS/MEREDITH 2004:507ff), and the *Complete Catalogue of Published Works*, published in 2006 as a common publication by all Arnold publishers (available from Faber Music, London). A new edition of Poulton's thematic catalogue will be published soon.

[3] About the term, role, and function of "film music" or "functional music" and their aesthetic singularity, cf. Eggebrecht 1999 (EGGEBRECHT 1999:157; 186-187), Schneider, N. J. 1997 (SCHNEIDER, N. J. 1997:49-55; 75-84), and Sloterdijk 1993 (SLOTERDIJK 1993:304-305). In Fuhr's account *Populäre Musik und Ästhetik* (*Popular Music and Aesthetics*) published in 2007, the negative adjunct regarding popular music prevailing particularly within the musicological and the cultural/philosophical approach are the starting point for any deliberations on the aesthetics of popular music (FUHR 2007:33-36); specifically on the issue of popular music as *Nicht-Kunst* ("Non-Art") (FUHR 2007:52 et seqq.).

[4] However, one must refrain here from discussing in more detail the issue of the perception of texts with a receptive intention – Cole, Harris/Meredith, and Jackson developed their interpretations of Arnold and created their images of him; now, the author of the present work

The question of novelty, or the „Dinge, die noch nicht gesagt worden sind" (Eco 2005:16) – *"thing(s) which have not already been said"–* gains central significance when reviewing the state of existing research. The provocative subtitle, *The Life and Music of Britain's Most Misunderstood Composer,* was indeed a deliberate choice by Harris and Meredith in 2004. On the one hand, it emphasises their opinion that Arnold's music is not perceived in a way that adequately reflects its quality. In this respect, the evaluation by the two authors is similar to the judgment made by Cole in 1989, although Cole still places him on a par with other composers:[5]

"...Malcolm Arnold has often been the victim, not so much of misrepresentation as of partial representation. He has been judged and categorised (as were Poulenc and Prokofiev before him) almost entirely on the strength of a few, much played, popular works..." (COLE 1989: vii).

On the other hand, Harris and Meredith consider Arnold's lack of acceptance as a composer within British musicology - an apt statement. Apart from the four works mentioned in the preceding paragraph and two works by Craggs (1998) and Poulton (1986) (which are rather designed as reference works or bibliographies), Arnold's name is always mentioned only in passing in the publications. This seems somewhat odd considering that he was knighted by Queen Elizabeth II and, furthermore, is among the British composers most frequently produced and recorded on CD in Great Britain.[6] With the exception of lexical articles in *The New Grove's Dictionary of Music* (compiled by Cole) and in the *MGG* music encyclopaedia (in which the entry is a translation of Cole's article), Arnold

is re-interpreting the aforementioned authors' works, a secondary step that poses the danger of distortion. This has previously happened, for instance, in the case of Adorno and his aesthetic theory, as Christine Eichel (EICHEL 1994:159-173) astutely concluded.

[5] It should be added that a composer who is "undiscovered" should not necessarily be declared a subject for research, without regard to other considerations, simply because only a few authors have written about him.

[6] The following are examples of scientific analyses of partial aspects of Arnold's music:BACH, E. S. (1991): A performance project on selected works of five composers. D.M.A. dissertation, University of British Columbia (Canada); HANNA, S. R. (1993): Analysis and performance of music for unaccompanied bassoon by Malcolm Arnold, Gordon Jacob, William Osborne, George Perle and Vincent Persichetti. D.M.A Eastman School of Music, University of Rochester, New York; HOFACRE, M. J. (1986): The use of tenor trombone in 20th century brass quintet music. D.M.A. dissertation, University of Oklahoma.

appears either peripherally as an element of musical analysis within a very limited, specific context, e.g., in individual analyses of works on brass music,[7] or in the context of studies on film music.

Arnold's first real orchestral composition, Larch Trees, opus 3, a tone poem for orchestra, dates from 1943, and his Symphony No. 1, opus 22, was composed in 1949.[8] While one cannot criticise Schaarwächter's attempt, in his detailed source study *Die britische Sinfonie 1914-1945* (SCHAARWÄCHTER 1994), Saremba's refusal to include Arnold in his compendium *Elgar, Britten und Co*, seems incomprehensible. A single, short quotation may reveal his real motives: ...Im englischsprachigen Kulturkreis fand er [Walton] viele kompetente Nachfolger. Komponisten wie der befreundete Malcolm Arnold (geb. 1921) konnten es sich gerade durch die Tantiemen von Welterfolgen wie der Musik zu dem Film Bridge on the River Kwai leisten, auch 'ambitioniertere' Orchester- und Bühnenwerke zu schreiben... (SAREMBA 1994:264). *"...In English-speaking cultural circles he [Walton] found many competent successors. Composers like his friend Malcolm Arnold (born in 1921) could also afford to write 'more ambitious' orchestral works and stage works because of the royalties he received for worldwide successes like the music for the film Bridge on the River Kwai..."*

Günter Moseler has pointed out a tendency toward the regionalisation and transformation of the symphonic form in Great Britain, and refers to Arnold's symphonies. His analysis of Arnold's second symphony, only one small paragraph, is marked by a short description of a single phenomena; he underlines, for example, Arnold's exposed use of the interval of a third in the 2nd Symphony and compares that to Nielsen's 4th and 5th Symphonies. If one agrees with this interpretation, Moseler's observations of Arnold's aesthetic position can be regarded as precise. He concludes:

„....die Kritik an seiner Musik betrifft besonders die ‚ernste' Gattung der Symphonie. Dies liegt zu einem gewissen Teil an seiner, durch biographische Umstände zusätzlich beeinflussten ästhetischen Zwischenpositionen, die zu einem nicht geringen Anteil eine buchstäblich unvermittelte Synthese populärmusikalischer Tendenzen mit dem traditionellen Charakter einer Symphonie...zum Stilprinzip erhoben hat..." (MOSELER 2002:202). *"... the criticism of his music especially concerns the 'serious' genre of the symphony. This has to do partly with his aesthetic positions, influenced to an extent by biographical circumstances in which Arnold has developed a literally abrupt synthesis of popular-musical tendencies within the traditional character of a symphony, raising this to an overall style principle..."* This shall be examined separately later in this study.

---

[7] Regarding the complexity of film music studies or reviews, some laudatory, some critical: ANON. (1958): 'Film music and beyond' in: Music Review, 19 (May 1958); Cole 1989 (COLE 1989:56-72); Jackson 2003 (JACKSON 2003:41-55) TALBERT, T. (1957/1958): 'Current Scores': in Film Music, 17 (Fall-Winter 1957-1958). Arnold's own comments about film music compositions are particularly interesting: ARNOLD, M. (1965): 'Film Music' in: Recorded Sound, no. 18 (April 1965): 328-334.

[8] Nevertheless, Schaarwächter mentions Malcolm Arnold's composition teacher, Gordon Jacob, *cf.* Schaarwächter 1994 (SCHAARWÄCHTER 1994:72-73; 314-315; 329).

In British musical historiography, there are other equally positive – though isolated – cases. Arnold Whittall's judgement in his full-scale study *Musical Composition in the Twentieth Century*, in which he classifies Arnold with Brian, Brax, and Rubbra as "British symphonist successors" (WHITTALL 1999:68), may not be correct in all stylistic cases. It does, however, testify to his ability to follow the precise context of British music.

At the same time, other British authors tend to evade the difficulty of classifying Arnold, who apparently felt pluralistically "at home" in all styles. They do not consider him a main character in the development of British contemporary classical music, thereby making it unnecessary to include him in, for example, Karolyi's book, *The Second British Musical Renaissance* (KAROLYI 1994:130).

Nevertheless, in Eco's opinion, the ostensible fact of an incorrect or insufficient perception of Arnold cannot serve as a singular argument for a scientific elaboration. What does meet his standard is the following premise: that the author will illustratively investigate Arnold's works and their applied compositional techniques, in detail, from a music-analytical as well as an aesthetic viewpoint. Conclusions will be drawn from the analysis that will, ideally, revise or complement the present image of Arnold. Arnold is much more than simply another representative of British "light classical music" – a term Cook and Pople use dismissively[9] (COOK /POPLE 2004:309-310). His music combines progressiveness and lightness in a very special way: without being arbitrary.

To address Eco's third and fourth demands, two statements must be made. According to Eco's third point, the question of the "usefulness" of a scientific paper, this has been already discussed by pointing towards the possibility of revising Arnold's image. His fourth demand, verification of conclusions, does not require additional explanation, either; it is guaranteed both by the author's argument and by a complete listing of all quoted sources. Hence, the author's methodology shall now be addressed, i.e., the necessity for an aesthetic discussion of compositional works as well as the compatibility and, above all, feasibility, of a simultaneous aesthetic and technical analysis.

European post-war contemporary music, especially German contemporary music, has been striving for a fresh start after the breakdown of its former totalitarian, imperial system. This process, which began at a predominantly technical level (composers began to write differently than they had before), has been underscored by a full-scale aesthetic discussion. Leading roles in this discussion were often awarded to centres like Donaueschingen and Darmstadt, but also included Cologne, Hamburg, and

---

[9] In Scowcroft's relatively new study, *British Light Music*, which includes 32 case studies on "light" composers, Arnold is not even explicitly mentioned. of. He appears only in the last chapter, "The Best of All of the Rest", and is mentioned there very briefly, imprecisely, and much too cursorily: "...A composer of nine symphonies and many concertos is surely a purveyor of 'serious' music, but...Arnold has never been afraid to write readily recognisable tunes...In any case, much of Arnold's generous output is classifiable as light music..." (SCOWCROFT 1997:102).

Munich. The movement was accompanied by philosophical ponderings of figures like Theodor Adorno. On the one hand, his statements had a strong impact on a whole class of composers; on the other hand, this meant hindrances for another class who still lived within the same generation.

The so-called "new simplicity" composers of the 1970s (Rihm, Trojahn, von Bose) have been the subject of research and have all taken part in the intellectual discussion about aesthetic views and their consequences on the composition process.[10] The composers' "simultaneous" participation in an aesthetic discussion and composition (the production of works) was instrinsic to twentieth-century European music history overall. Therefore, one cannot disregard it in any aesthetic consideration of such an authentic European composer as Arnold.

Great Britain's secure position after the Allied victory in World War II meant that it did not have to rebuild its empire, in comparison to Germany, which had been destroyed (a statement completely free of any historical resentments). This also meant that composers in Great Britain considered "progress" in a different context from composers in continental Europe.[11] Adorno's idea of the „Verbrauchtheit des Materials" *(the "worn-outness" of the material itself)* therefore became important only at the point when young English composers understood the development of the second Viennese school and integrated it audibly into their works. In this context, we can cite composers like Peter Maxwell Davies,[12] Harrison Birtwistle (both 1934 –), and Alexander Goehr (1932 –).[13]

It may be too early in this paper to demonstrate how being conscious of traditions and sensitive to the "new" can be reconciled in the case of Malcolm Arnold. But the general characterisation of his peculiar situation in Great Britain can be underlined by Dibelius, who described his, also quite typical for contemporary continental-Europeans and too all-inclusive perception of Great Britain:

„...Die englische Musik muss sich eben - anders als auf dem Festland - nicht gegen ein kulturelles Überangebot, gegen eine abgestumpfte Saturiertheit oder auch nur gegen die Klischees der Vorgänger durchsetzen. Aggressive oder oppositionelle Beigaben bleiben aus, weil sie nicht notwendig sind. Das musikalische Feld ist ja relativ unbesetzt, und wer genügend Elan hat, wird es schon bestellen können. Dies wäre also eins der Charakteristika englischer Musik: ein gewisser Konservatismus, der aber keineswegs verstockt oder rückständig zu sein braucht, sondern eher als Regulativ gegenüber forcierter Modernität wirkt und zu einiger stilistischer Unbefangenheit erzieht..." (DIBELIUS 1998:291-292). *"...English music must not assert itself – contrary to the situation on the mainland – against a cultural oversupply, against blunted saturation or even against predecessor's stereotypes. Aggressive or oppositional additions are*

---

[10] The best examples may be the extensive analytic, aesthetic, and philosophical writings of Wolfgang Rihm, Nikolaus A. Huber, and Helmut Lachenmann.

[11] The fact that this can be only **one** factor regarding contemporary music is obvious, cf. the author's statements in chapters 4 and 6.

[12] Davies's serial techniques can be observed in his trumpet sonata (1955) and in *Pieces for Piano* (1956).

[13] Composers like Searle and Wellesz were accepted in England less for their compositions, based upon the twelve-tone technique, than for their writings or their work as musicologists.

*missing because they are not necessary. The musical field is relatively
unoccupied, and someone who has enough vigour will be able to cope with
that. This would be described as one of the characteristic features of
English music: a certain conservatism which is, however, by no means
obdurate or does not have to be out-of-date but rather works as a
regulator toward forced modernity leading to some stylistic
impartiality..."*

Although Dibelius's appraisal is completely appropriate with
regard to the more conservative styles, he completely underestimates
politico-cultural market structures. His analysis seems to be strongly
influenced by the aestheticised situation of German music after 1945. His
sense that there were no tendencies towards progress in English
compositional writing can be disproved by the works of the above-
mentioned three composers, known as the "Manchester School".[14] The
special aesthetic situation of the British avant-garde as opposed to the
postmodernists will be discussed more precisely later; therefore, Dibelius's
statement must, for the moment, be viewed in only relative terms.

Arnold seldom expresses his thoughts on his compositional
technique in literary form. Only a few of his personal writings and essays,
statements, and interviews on his aesthetic stance remain. However, this
does not mean that an aesthetic discussion is not necessary. Indeed, in the
following thesis, aesthetic concepts will be further discussed in terms of
Arnold's compositional style in order to categorise him within twentieth-
century British contemporary music. This study is in no way intended as a
general treatise about the absolute value of Arnold's music and symphonic
works.

In the introductory and methodological remarks in Angerer's
study on musical aestheticism applied to the later works of Skrjabin
(ANGERER 1984:13-32), Angerer has clearly recognised the danger of a
purely technical, formal musical analysis.[15] He describes this as

---

[14] Just as representatives of the new simplicity had to defend themselves, English composers
neglected to be classified as the so-called "Manchester School". This term does not have
anything to do with their music, but refers to where Birtwistle, Davies, and Goehr studied.
[15] It is worth mentioning that the demand for "openness" within musicological research has
been one of the main issues in Angerer's career as a professor of music; in 1998, he
underscored its importance during the jubilee celebrating 100 years of musicology in Vienna
and considers the politico-cultural context: „*....Fast nie ist es einem Musikwissenschaftler
gelungen, über die Grenzen seiner Disziplin innovativ und anregend zu wirken. Namen wie
Panofsky oder C.S. Lewis, Blanchot oder Sedlmayr, Gombrich oder Barthes, G. Steiner oder
de Man hat unser Fach nur drei Autoren entgegenzusetzen, die allgemein bekannt sind und
von hohem intellektuellen Niveau sind: Hanslick, Adorno und Alejo Carpentier...Diese noble
Zurückhaltung allem gegenüber, was negativ formuliert modisch, in positiver Wendung: über
die Fachgrenzen hinaus aktuell und spannend sein könnte, ist eine direkte Folge der speziellen
kulturhistorischen Bedingungen, unter denen das akademische Fach Musikwissenschaft vor
hundert Jahren begründet wurde...*" (ANGERER 1998:37-38). "...A musicologist has almost
never succeeded in appearing innovative and stimulating the borders of his discipline. Names like
Panofsky or C.S. Lewis, Blanchot or Sedlmayr, Gombrich or Barthes, G. Steiner or de Man can
only be contrasted with three authors in our field who are known in general and who show a high
intellectual level: Hanslick, Adorno, and Alejo Carpentier...This noble restraint against everything
that could be negatively formulated, fashionable, but positively stated, could be exciting, and is a
direct result of the special cultural-historical conditions under which the academic field of
musicology was founded a hundred years ago..."

„Ungenügen an der Ausschließlichkeit der musikalischen Analyse und ihrer musikhistorischen Verwendung" (ANGERER 1984:29) *("dissatisfaction with the exclusivity of musical analysis and its use in music history")* and develops, drawing on Adler's style definition and Bürger's 1974 "theory of the avant-garde", the idea of applying analytical methods, aesthetic viewpoints, and compositional-technical questions equally when assessing a work. He writes: „...Ist der Ästhetizismus das Stadium totaler Verfügbarkeit über Kunstmittel, deren geschichtliche, inhaltliche Bestimmungen weitgehend ausgeschaltet werden, muss die Analyse solcher Kunstwerke bei ihrer Technik ansetzen. Untersuchungen dieser Art bleiben allerdings keine rein technisch-formalen. Die krude Trennung von Inhalt und Form ist keine Forderung der Sache, sondern gehört selber einer vergangenen Epoche der kunsttheoretischen Reflexion auf einem bestimmten, dem Ästhetizismus vorangegangenen Stand der Kunstproduktion an. Der Inbegriff aller formalen Momente des Kunstwerks ist das 'künstlerische Material'..." (ANGERER 1984:28) *("...If aestheticism is the stage of complete availability of art that means that its historical content regulations are to a great extent switched off, the analysis of such pieces of art must begin with their technique. However, investigations of this kind do not remain purely technical-formal. The unsatisfactory separation of content and form is not the only demand in this case, but it does itself belong to the past epoch of art-theoretical reflection on a certain state preceding the aestheticism of art production. The perfect example of all formal moments of a piece of art is the 'artistic material'...").*

In this context, we can certainly agree with his argument. Observing a scientific object within the "whole" frame, working out its artistic material, and thoroughly reviewing the artistic material clearly belong to the current canons of scientific methods. Moreover, his statement that an imbalance between musical analysis and more cursory aesthetic discussion would take place much too often (ANGERER 1984:29) can be hardly contradicted.[16]

He connects this with the following demand: "...[es] schon auf den Versuch an[käme], das Emotionale oder Irrationale an unserer verehrten Kunst thematisch werden zu lassen wie die einst so beliebte 'musikalische Logik'. Andere Disziplinen wie Geschichte und Ethnologie...haben das ja nicht ganz erfolglos auch versucht..." (ANGERER 1998:42). "... (it) would already [depend] on the attempt to let the emotional or irrational in our honoured art become thematic, as happened in the case of the very much liked 'musical logic'. Other disciplines like history and ethnology...did indeed succeed quite successfully..."

[16] Ridley points out that this problem can be likewise found in parts of philosophy: "...[the philosophy of art]. It's an issue about where the emphasis falls. Is the emphasis on the word 'philosophy' or is the emphasis on the word 'art' I think a lot of aesthetics is one with the

In the same framework, however, in which Angerer contemplates the cooperation of both spheres (aesthetic discussion and musical analysis), he treats them, within the scope of his own research on Skrjabin, as "reactionary" at a formal level.

This methodology chapter is followed by two very specific, but, for the most part, music-analysis oriented chapters: conclusions on Skrjabin's later style, and a case study of Skrjabin's 9th sonata for piano, opus 68. He curiously supplies an aesthetic discussion later, in the form of a chapter dealing with fetishism (1984:105 et seqq.). Let us ask in a very subtle way: doch keine „musikalische Analyse...im Hinblick auf größere Zusammenhänge konzipiert..." (ANGERER 1984:29) *(no "musical analysis conceived...within the frame of a larger context...?"*

The assessment and labelling of this procedure as "reactionary" is superficial. If one considers it more closely, its advantages become obvious. Executing such an aesthetic discussion of every single work, separately and immediately within each text, would become a never-ending process. It would also be interwoven with the topic itself. Indeed, it may be tempting, for the purposes of a general study, to research a topic from all possible points of view and to treat it as interdisciplinary, utilising all humanities-related professional disciplines. This could be a very interesting challenge for every author, but the precision of every statement would suffer because while musical analytical conclusions are tangible, aesthetic conclusions, even within the framework of an excellent argument, are still subjective value judgements.

The latter are necessary, however, so that the author can position himself in relation to the research subject. Nevertheless, aesthetic conclusions cannot be used as a substitute for any scientific statements; they can serve only to complement them.

If we now return to Arnold, let us listen to another "Arnold", Arnold Schönberg. His definition of style will accompany this research from now on:

"The positive and negative rules may be deduced from a finished work as constituents of its style. Every man has fingerprints of his own, and

---

emphasis on the philosophy, and by that I mean that the motivation or the occasion for thinking about art is prompted by or conducted with the use of conclusions, techniques or methods that have been developed in other parts of philosophy..." (RIDLEY 2002:64).

every craftsman's hand has its personality; out of such subjectivity grow the traits which comprise the style of the finished product...

Style is the quality of a work and is based on natural conditions, expressing him who produced it..." (SCHÖNBERG [1946] 1984:121).

2. The Myth of Invention: A Case Study on Arnold's Composition Process and Orchestration Technique

"...One should be able to play the piano..." Friedrich Schröder

We have a tendency to think in perception archetypes. If a person is asked to name an oval form, there is a statistically high probability that he will think of an "egg". This is not simply a result of the interrogative questionnaire technique used. To us, an "egg" represents an associative value of experiences, and thus acts as an archetype to simplify classification of the abstract concept "oval".[17]

It is obvious that composers tend to adapt this image in their self-presentation, as do authors, philosophers, and scientists in their own statements about composers. The image of Beethoven inventing music while walking through a forest is understandably appealing to an idle composer, but Mozart seemed to be dumbfounded and helpless when asked about his creative process.[18] Arnold didn't neglect that image, either, as he answered Murray Schafer's question in 1963 about how his ideas would arise: "They [the ideas] may come any time. I don't keep a notebook for them, because I can always remember them. I find they accumulate and develop automatically, no matter what I may be doing. My mind seems to pick them up like a rolling snowball and eventually there are enough for an entire work" (SCHAFER 1963:152).

Along with the idea of spontaneous creative activity goes the image that an opus and all of its aspects would originate at that moment of inspiration. Above all, its final *Gestalt* would be predetermined. The composer would only need to use a pen to establish his pre-imagined setting (as Kant would say) in order to create an "opus" for all times.[19]

As enticing as the image may appear, it does not generally correspond to the reality of composition. The composition process is marked by various stages. The immediate initial idea, derived from Husserl's directness and not rationally explicable or tangible to outsiders, is followed by clear work steps: mental composing activity, sometimes combined with sound realisation at an instrument, sketching ideas, and, if

---

[17] On the general subject of perception and the question of symbols: *cf.* Cassirer (CASSIRER 2000:108-111); on the intersubjectivity of the world: *cf.* Husserl (HUSSERL 1981:210-215).
[18] We must avoid discussing problems raised by the fact that this image could also be disproved by counterexamples – Gustav Mahler composing at the desk in his summer house or Igor Stravinsky, who always preferred to compose physically at the piano. The examples mentioned serve their purpose within the argument.
[19] "...Kunst wird von der Natur, wie Tun (facere) vom Handeln oder Wirken überhaupt (agere), und das Produkt und die Folge des erstern als Werk (opus) von dem letztern als Wirkung (effectus) unterschieden..." "... *Art is differentiated from nature, as "activity" (facere) or "effect" (agere) in general, and the product or the piece of creative work (opus) is distinguished from its effect (effectus)*" (KANT 1995:237).

necessary, the production of a short score with the purpose of finalising a full score. Of course, these processes represent an idealised composition process. However, let's imagine: provided that the first inspiration does not turn out to be viable in practice, or that the composer wants to modify his original idea and develop it further, what shall he do? The image of an artistic opus, originating in a purposeful, unique, and singular act is naive, even if this realisation means that the idealised genius myth must be discarded.

Furthermore, the question of whether a composer needs a "helping" instrument for his composition process is irrelevant for any initial aesthetic assessment of the composition, regardless of whether a composer uses an instrument, composes completely in his mind, writes a short score or goes directly to the full orchestral score. The value of a piece cannot be measured by its genesis, only by its outcome. It is also striking that the approaches of various composers of the eighteenth, nineteenth, or even twentieth centuries hardly differ, even if such different composers as Mozart, Hindemith or Stravinsky are discussed.

Volker Scherliess has investigated Stravinvky in depth. Even if his is only a representative study that cannot be applied to any single composer, he describes Stravinsky's creative acts and refers to original sources (scores) as well as documents and comments Stravinsky made to his long-standing employee and protégé Robert Craft: „...[vollzog sich] Strawinskys Arbeitsweise...grundsätzlich in einem Dreischritt:

Spontane Einfälle wurden in einem der Skizzenbücher, die er zeitlebens führte, oder auf losen Blättern, Briefkuverts oder ähnlichem, was gerade vorhanden war, notiert. (Für den *Sacre du Printemps* etwa sind ein Telegrammformular und eine Restaurantrechnung erhalten...

Dann stellte er die Einzelskizzen in klaviermäßiger Anordnung oder als mehr oder minder ausführliches Particell zusammen...

Als dritter Arbeitsgang – die Schritte lassen sich nicht immer genau trennen – wurden dann die Einzelelemente zusammengefasst, ,kom-poniert', d.h. in eine bestimmte Reihenfolge gebracht, wobei vielfach Umstellungen, Streichungen und Einfügungen vorgenommen wurden. Dies geschah meist in Form eines detailliert ausgeführten Particells, zum Teil in mehrfachen Versionen und oft schon in einer Fassung, die sich kaum von der endgültigen Partitur unterscheidet. Danach folgte die Reinschrift der Partitur...“ (SCHERLIESS 1993:167-168).

"...Stravinsky's method of composition [took place] basically in three steps:

Spontaneous inspirations were noted in his sketch books or on loose sheets, envelopes, or on any similar drawing sheets that were available (he used, for instance, a telegram form and a restaurant bill for Sacre du Printemps ... *Then he put together these single sketches and arranged them in a setting for piano; a more or less detailed short score followed.... As a third step – the steps cannot always be described separately – the*

26

single elements were put together (in the sense of com-ponere*) in a certain order but often rearranged and adapted. Replacements were made, too. These are prominent in most of his detailed short scores, are found in multiple versions, and are often found in settings that hardly differ from the final orchestral full score.[20] Afterwards, a final copy of the score was created... ".*

Returning to the myth of Arnold's genius, a large part of the available scientific research on Malcolm Arnold has evoked a similar mythical picture of his composition process. Apart from Cole, who does not speculate on this subject and who instead focuses on the music-theoretical points of Arnold's pre-1989 compositions, Jackson and Meredith and Harris try to evoke a similar type of genius image very much in the sense of Kant's claim (KANT 1995:421-243). These contributions lead to a construction and mythologisation of Arnold. However, the actual sources used for this study do not support this image.

Jackson's image of a highly gifted composer who has perfect pitch and does not really need tools, but instead only uses his mind, is not my main point of criticism. Arnold's approach can be proven by his own comments as well as by those of his friends (JACKSON 2003:4-5). Jackson first examines works from Arnold's early (approximately pre-1945/1950) and middle phases (approximately pre-1978)[21] based on their visual look, their "optic". He compares several later scores, cleanly written and with the highest aesthetic optic claim, with the (also) handwritten final copy of the *Phantasy for Strings (Vita Abundans)* (1941). This manuscript creates an impression of rashness.[22] Jackson draws the conclusion that this opus was created in a compressed and concentrated moment. In Jackson's opinion, however, it is not a unified whole, because there are scribbles and corrections in the original manuscript: "...The sixteen pages of manuscript are crammed full of notes that seem in danger of falling off the page...There are certain crossings-out and blotches, which point to a work written under pressure. He was obviously composing straight onto the paper ...".

Jackson concludes that Arnold's composition process tended to correspond more or less to that idealised image of the creation of music within the composer's mind: "...In later life he would write into ink a work that was already fully formed in his head. With this piece [*Phantasy for Strings*] we can see the process happening ..." (JACKSON 2003:13).

The source material reviewed, including material from the Arnold Estate[23] as well as some publicly accessible material, leads to a completely different conclusion regarding Arnold's composition process than what Jackson described. Arnold's strategy of creating an opus as a complete and unified whole seems to be maintained – only marginal

---

[20] This detail will be also observed in later analysis of the *Overture of Robert Kett*.

[21] Regarding the categorisation of Arnold's works into early and middle phases, consult chapters three and four.

[22] The work was created under pressure in only five days and was delivered to the panel of the Cobbett Prize for composition, which Arnold won.

[23] This material has not been published yet; it was first reviewed by the author in January/February 2006, Attleborough, Norfolk, UK.

scribbles can be found. In contrast, he prepares decidedly short piano scores (particells), mostly arranged in the setting of two to three systems or in the form of a melody with orchestral accompaniment. Notes on orchestration are rarely found, and the draft short score of the *Four Welsh Dances* even contains the perfidious remark "different orchestration 2nd time" without stating Arnold's proposed implementation.

Even Harris and Meredith believe in their propagated image of Arnold directly writing into a full score rather than using several steps. In fact, they clearly work out how Arnold followed the latter procedure (two steps: particell and later orchestration) in the case of his 9th Symphony. They also note that this conclusion cannot be applied to all of his symphonic works. However, they strangely contradict themselves in their statement, "...The Ninth Symphony did not follow the same compositional method as the preceding eighth, because he flinched at the prospect of writing into full score" (HARRIS/MEREDITH 2004:454). On page 383 of their book, an original particell of the 8th Symphony is printed, clearly revealing that Arnold used three systems to sketch out the beginning of his 8th symphony (*sic*). Even if Arnold did not sketch out the **complete** work as he did with his 9th, we must consider this a sketching process. Harris and Meredith tend to generalise, negating the concept of a working process instead of the genius myth.

The short scores (particells) therefore serve as drafts for a later orchestration – an approach that Richard Wagner and Alban Berg[24] also cultivated. All of these constructs lead to a clear statement. The general image of Arnold's composition process as a unique and immediate one-step process cannot be sustained if one investigates Arnold's whole oeuvre. The myth needs to be revised. The greater the number of accurate sources available (e.g. primary and secondary sources like sketches, short scores, fair copies or galley proofs), the better one can reconstruct the genesis of a work.

In the following analysis, two orchestral works, the *Four Irish Dances*, opus 126 (1986) and the *Overture Robert Kett*, opus 141 (1988) will be illustratively examined in regard to their composition process.[25] The author will draw his conclusions from original sketches that are available in the Malcolm Arnold Manuscripts Loan Collection at The Royal College of Music in London, or that belong to the Arnold Estate. He will primarily discuss drafts (publishers' lithographs and Arnold's handwritten final manuscripts) as well as available published scores.

Bruce Ellis Benson interestingly points towards the aesthetics of the composing process as well as to the definition and extension of the concept itself in his study, *The Improvisation of Musical Dialogue: A Phenomenology of Music*, published in

---

[24] In 2000, Rainer Schwob pointed out the importance for a composer to produce short scores as a basis for later orchestration and as a tool for spontaneous realisation in the creative process of inventing and developing ideas. It is striking that even Alban Berg used this method for the 12-tone related compositions (SCHWOB 2000).

[25] The author selected the following two pieces because the works are particularly informative about Arnold's process of composing music.

2003. Referring to Gadamer (1990[6]), Goehr (1992), Ingarden (1972[4]) and Wolterstorff (1980), he develops the idea that composition and improvisation, two spheres often seen as diametrically opposed, have more in common than it would appear and that they depend on each other (BENSON 2003).

Considering a statement made by Wolterstorff describing a musician improvising ad hoc at an instrument and writing down his improvisation when at home (Benson chooses the organ as an example), he underscores that this instrumentalist has to face an aesthetic problem; he is "in a quandary". He has neither composed an opus by performing an improvisation, nor has he composed while improvising. Benson first expounds upon the problem of a sharp dividing line between composition and improvisation, and hypothesises as follows: "...I will argue that the process by which a work comes into existence is *best* described as improvisatory at its very core, not merely the act of composing but also the acts of performing and listening. In my view, improvisation is not something that *precedes* composition (*pace* Wolterstorff) or stands outside and opposed to composition. Instead, I think that the activities that we call 'composing' and 'performing' are essentially improvisational in nature, even though improvisation takes many different forms in each activity. As we shall see, if my claim is correct, the beginnings and endings of musical pieces may indeed be 'real' (as opposed to merely 'imagined'), but they are often messy. *Exactly* where and when they begin and end may not be easy to specify..." (BENSON 2003:2-3).

Furthermore, Benson takes the classical model of a composer as a creator, interpreter and performer into consideration – describing the composer as a "mouthpiece" (BENSON 2003: 13) – and underscores his point by referring to Beethoven and Rossini. While Beethoven defined his symphonies as "inviolable musical texts" and claimed that these texts had to be executed in an almost exegetic way,[26] a work by Rossini could be instead regarded as sort of a "recipe" or instruction for a later performance. "...What accounts for this difference is that Rossini thought of his music not as a 'work' but as something that came into existence only in the moment of performance. In practice, this meant that a piece of music had no fixed identity and so could be adapted for a given performance. Thus, the performer had an important role in the creation of musical works. Even more important, it was not the work that was given precedence; rather, the work (and thus the composer) was in effect a partner in dialogue with performers and listeners..." (BENSON 2003:16-17).

Benson concludes from the highly virtuosic singer-bravura layout revealed in a Rossini aria that an interpretation of a composition contains core elements of improvisation. Although he recognises the differences between the concepts of interpretation and composition, he underlines their dependence on each other: "...On the one hand, improvisation seems at least to be a kind of extemporaneous composition in that it does not seem to be an 'interpretation' of something that already exists. In this sense, it differs from performance...A performance is essentially an *interpretation* of something that already exists, whereas improvisation presents us with something that only comes into being in the moment of its presentation..." (BENSON 2003:24).

Nevertheless, he outlines two important points. He postulates that no composer would just create something from nothing (ex nihilo); a composer would instead choose from known traditions and social conditions in order to **improvise** ("...Composers never create *ex nihilo*, but instead 'improvise': sometimes on tunes that

---

[26] On the general variability of dynamics and tempo and in contrast to Ravel's statement "Il ne faut pas interpreter ma musique, il faut la réaliser", *cf.* Schuller (SCHULLER 1998:15-51); Schuller's view on Beethoven's 5th (1998:109ff) and 7th symphonies (1998:231ff).

already exist, but more frequently and importantly on the traditions in which they work..." [BENSON 2003:25]). [27]

Composition could be therefore described as the selection process within these frames of tradition in order to create an independent opus. Benson describes composing as "...the process of selection ..." (2003:69). This process cannot be viewed out of context.[28]

He vehemently contradicts the idea of an isolated composer neglecting all traditions:[29] "...What is 'appropriate' for a classical composer *today* is remarkably different today from what it was two centuries ago. Think of what Haydn could have written and what say, Charles Koechlin was able to write in... discourses (or practices) have certain texts - and thus, composers - that are taken to be authoritative... A composer, then, does not compose in a social vacuum but within a rather firmly defined social practice..." (2003:42)

At the same time, he criticises the idea of a first-and-final setting of an opus. Kant's idea of the artist addicted to art (a sort of "l'art pour l'art") clearly conflicted with the real reasons that a composer finished a score. This construct would often lead to a primarily public misperception of a composer's approach. If a composer authoritatively completed his opus, he would not usually do so for artistic reasons, but rather because of external musical factors like an upcoming deadline for a performance or publication (2003:66). For example, if Schubert had completed his Unfinished Symphony in three movements, it could have been described as Schubert's Finished Symphony – but it might also have been "robbed" of its defining features (2003:67).

In terms of Arnold and Benson, Arnold indeed admits that he could find new inspiration from improvisation. However, this could not be described as an act of composition: "I do not compose at the piano. I find it interrupts the flow of thought if I have to stop to consider what my hands are doing on the keyboard...I will add that I have spent many hours improvising at the piano, exploring for new harmonic and melodic sounds, and I regard this a valuable exercise; but it is not composing, and any discoveries I have made through these experiments only come out later and subconsciously in my work..." (SCHAFER 1963: 152).

Indeed, Benson can be credited as having presented philosophical proof of the substantial similarity of the two hemispheres – provided that we follow his argument and agree with its delineations. However, he has worked out very clearly that the vague act that is the genesis of a piece of art is strongly accompanied by

---

[27] Benson's view can interestingly be compared to Riehn's concept of composition as a "Mosaik von Zitaten" (*"a mosaic of quotations"*): „...Jede Komposition baut sich als Mosaik von Zitaten auf, jede Komposition ist Absorption und Transformation einer anderen Komposition. Jede Sequenz *schafft* sich selbst in Bezug auf eine andere, die aus einem anderen Korpus stammt, so dass jede Sequenz doppelt orientiert ist: zum Akt der Erinnerung und zum Akt der Aufforderung hin..." (RIEHN 1998:68). *"...Any composition is based on a mosaic of quotations; any composition is an absorption and transformation of another composition. Every sequence creates itself in relation to another one coming from another body, so that every sequence has two orientations: one realated to the act of the recollection/memory and another to the act of the request..."*

[28] Malcolm Arnold is quoted: "My string quartets and symphonies are the story of my life"; see *Complete Catalogue of Published Works*, available from Faber Music, London.

[29] Let us remember Kandinsky's claim: „...Jedes Kunstwerk ist Kind seiner Zeit, oft ist es Mutter unserer Gefühle.So bringt jede Kulturperiode eine eigene Kunst zustande, die nicht mehr wiederholt werden kann...Wir können z. B. unmöglich wie alte Griechen fühlen und innerlich leben...Eine derartige Nachahmung gleicht den Nachahmung der Affen..." (KANDINSKY 1912:21). *"... Every piece of art is a child of its times, often it is a mother of our feelings. Thus, every cultural period creates its own art which cannot be repeated...We cannot possibly feel, e.g., like the ancient Greeks and live internally....Such imitation resembles the imitation of monkeys...".*

questions about practical considerations – usually something a composer does not like to admit.[30]

We will now analyse the *Four Irish Dances*, opus 138 (1986).[31]

These sketches consist of a total of eight pages: a cover page, a draft short score (first setting), and six successive short score pages summarising the full orchestra on two systems (piano system notation = piano short score).

In the piano short score, the main subject, based upon the pentatonic D-minor scale (D, F, G, A, C), is at first fully sketched out. Arnold further outlines a chord ostinato pattern of two bars that is later excluded by Arnold. A D-minor seventh-ninth chord, lasting one bar, is followed by a G-minor seventh chord of the same duration; the chords are rhythmically emphasised through their syncopated setting.

The manuscript is clearly legible – although it is handwritten, all entries, with the exception of the bar lines, seem to have been made without the use of a ruler. Additional corrections like scribbles of cresc. markings or a scribble of a complete bar are found in the fourth movement (vivace), though only twice. The short score indicates a stringent composition process – Arnold seems to express clear thoughts that have already been formed in his mind and that only need to be written on paper.[32]

Arnold consistently uses rehearsal letters in all movements, and he notes articulations and dynamics. However, it is very interesting that the score lacks any notes on its orchestration. This can be interpreted at first as an arbitrariness concerning the selection of tone colours that may be rejected, if one precisely compares the short score with the later full score. The structural layout of the composition reveals that Arnold prefers syntactically well-known periodic forms, usually consisting of eight bars. Besides, in this work he does not incorporate a lot of contrapuntal texture; it is mainly a two-layer setting (a melody layer and a harmony layer, or simple two-part-textures, *cf.* the fourth movement). It is therefore obvious that he does not need a complicated short score arrangement with many annotations; the basic layout found within the sketches of the *Four Irish Dances* provides enough information for the later process of orchestration – although this sketch approach is in contrast to Arnold's early orchestral works. The final orchestration (full score) of every movement shall now be systematically examined and analysed.

---

[30] Danuser's article collection, *Vom Einfall zum Kunstwerk (From the Inspiration to the Piece of Art)* is a very valuable collection of contributions about the compositional creative process, covering very different composers such as Debussy, Puccini, Pfitzner, Schönberg, and others. Debussy's secret preservation *cf.* Groth 1993 (GROTH 1993:23-25); in contrast, discusses Siegfried Matthus's too idealistic and almost flowery self-description *cf.* Matthus 1993 (MATTHUS 1993:396-398).
[31] Source: Arnold Estate.
[32] In this context: mea culpa Jackson...

Figure 1 *Four Irish Dances*, original short score, page 1

(Reproduced by kind permission of the Arnold Estate.)

First movement: The two-bar harmonic ostinato is repeated without any changes by part of the brass section within the first ten bars (the chord-layer is found in the trumpets; bass-notes in the bass trombone and tuba). The bass line is also supported by the violoncello/contrabasso section and by the bassoons. At letter A, this ostinato structure moves to the strings, rhythmically marginally modified in the second bar. The eight-bar main subject is presented in octave-unisons and is found not to be particularly differentiated in the strings (violins and violas) or in the woodwinds (flutes, oboes, and clarinets). At letter B, the listener is confronted with an interesting change in the chord structure. While the main subject is stated in the piccolo flute, Arnold virtually "exchanges" the bass notes within the harmonic two-bar ostinato. He also adds pizzicato-bass tones in the contrabasses to round up the overall impression; these small adjustments reveal Arnold's mastery of orchestral effects. This texture is further joined by a motion of descending minor thirds in the harp supporting the percussive impact of the military rhythm found in the tenor drum. In C and D, the subject is repeated, now in a full symphonic scoring.

It is striking that Arnold does not return to the original bass-line structure developed in A. Instead he retains B's structure, which leads to the following conclusion: what has been modified once will not be modified again.

By means of this simple compositional procedure/technique – one might even call them "cheats" in this case – Arnold creates new harmonic tensions within a constant melody, and a compositional "break" occurs. He has not just composed another new or old, stylised Irish folk dance. It is a real piece of art that demands that its sophisticated –although simple – structure be perceived by its recipients.

Arnold did not find it necessary to note this structural effect on the harmony – the accompanying chords remain unchanged, although in this context, this new bass-tone relation leads to a new structural harmonic effect – found within his sketches. In the descant voice, he only notates the melody, whereas in the lower system, he only notates the fundamental bass notes. He did not copy the two-bar chord-ostinato over and over again.

Figure 2 *Four Irish Dances*, **original short score, page 2**

(Reproduced by kind permission of the Arnold Estate.)

Finding such a high degree of compositional reflection, even within such a tonal and structurally simplistic composition, is surprising. Arnold should therefore be regarded as more than a talented "craftsman" who orchestrated short scores to full scores by simply copying note-for-note. As a composer, he is an artist.

Figure 3 *Four Irish Dances*, **full score, letter** B **: the new bass line**

Second movement: Arnold assigns the content of the short score
to clear instrumental groups within the full score, maintaining the same
registers and octave ranges used in the short score. In the Introduction and
in section A, he assigns the music to the string section. Interestingly, the
viola section is completely neglected. In section B, the structure in the
strings is assigned to the oboe (doubled in the harp), the clarinet, and a
bassoon in the context of a three-part texture. There are no overlapping
techniques in A and B, but five bars after B, the C-major chord in the

strings overlaps with the woodwind section, creating an interesting melding effect. It is important in this context that four bars before C, Arnold does not change the voicing structure. He literally copies the voicing structure of the piano short score and scores it within the string section. In conclusion, Arnold emphasises content and emotional expression; in other words, he emphasises the actual notes and not the voicing structure that could have been adjusted for use by the strings.

Figure 4 *Four Irish Dances*, original sketch, page 3

(Reproduced by kind permission of the Arnold Estate.)

Third Movement: The third movement, as presented in the piano short score, consists of exactly one page. It is a three-part texture, made up of a melody layer and a rhythmicised chord layer. When one compares the piano short score with the full score, it becomes obvious that the same octave ranges and register layout from the piano short score are used in the full orchestral layout. However, it might be said that Arnold, apart from the special tone colour of the solo piccolo in its very low register (see letter A), does not follow any higher orchestration principle in this approach – unless one considers the formula of this change of instrumentation itself as a special moment.

Figure 5 *Four Irish Dances*, original sketch, page 4

(Reproduced by kind permission of the Arnold Estate.)

Fourth movement: The vitality of the vivace beginning set in 9/8 and the main subject scored in unisons suggests a full-scale fugue in the style of Britten's final fugue in his *Young Person's Guide to the Orchestra*. But the actual instrumentation is hidden behind the two-part texture. Arnold wants to use as many combinations of melding sounds as possible. He succeeds in his typical style by creating changes in colour and tension – see in particular the virtuoso as well as the high-horn passages from letter B onward. At letter D, the full orchestra is reduced quite astonishingly to a flute duet; the same can be observed for the duet between the first and second violins from G. Despite its two-part texture, the pieced ends in a

37

full orchestral tutti. The scanty melodic structure is here spread very effectively by the use of unison octaves.

Figure 6 *Four Irish Dances*, original sketch, page 5

(Reproduced by kind permission of the Arnold Estate.)

The *Four Irish Dances* are extremely short and cannot be compared to the rather monstrous and, considering their more interesting and more diverse orchestration, pompous *English Dances* (*Set I, opus 27* [1950] as well as *Set II, opus 33* [1951]).

The *Four Irish Dances* represent the most varied facets of Arnold's style, in particular that of his later orchestral works: a trend towards the reduction, the use of two to three-part textures, Arnold's personal view that any reduced structure should likewise be expressed in a reduced orchestration.

It is of major importance that Arnold's later composition process is carried out in several interdependent steps which nevertheless need to be seen as separate processes. First drafts are followed, if necessary, by piano short scores, mostly on two or three systems, implying the main pieces of information as notes, structure of the accompaniment, dynamics, and articulations. The process of orchestration is then carried out as a final **separate** step. This procedure does indeed have both advantages and disadvantages. An advantage is that Arnold can concentrate on the opus-immanent "essentials", but a disadvantage is that he cannot always pay enough attention to careful orchestration, which was always one of the main characteristics of Arnold's early orchestral works. Indeed, this new type of orchestration also has exciting moments.[33] It is relieved of any unnecessary glamour and "effects" in the attitude of Richard Strauss's *Rosenkavalier*.[34]

---

[33] The author will examine this in depth in the case of the 9th Symphony.

[34] On the aesthetic evaluation of an orchestration and on the impact of an orchestration full of effects: *cf.* Jost (JOST 2004:40-46; 76-77; 106-111; 121-125).

Figure 7 *Four Irish Dances*, original sketch, page 6 (final page)

(Reproduced by kind permission of the Arnold Estate.)

The *Overture Robert Kett*[35], opus 141, composed in 1988, is a very interesting piece and a valuable source of research material. It is one of the last pieces Arnold ever composed. Also, by referring to his extremely precise sketches and drafts[36] we can understand a) which

---

[35] Robert Kett was a Norfolk landowner. Born in 1492, he came into conflict with King Edward VI; his misinterpretation of a royal act led to a march on Norwich with 16,000 supporters. The riots that he organised later failed, and Kett was executed. For a historical overview: *cf.* http://www.spartacus.schoolnet.co.uk/TUDkett.htm, downloaded on 3/16/2007, *cf.* http://www.bbb.co.uk/legacies/myths_legends/england/norfolk/article_1.shtml, downloaded on 3/16/2007. On the genesis of the work itself, Harris/Meredith and Jackson only reveal marginal pieces of information (JACKSON 2003:202), (HARRIS/MEREDITH 2004:475).

[36] Arnold only sketched the short score until letter M. However, the short score evokes the notion that he simply stopped sketching out the development, rather than that pages had been lost. Therefore, the sketched short score consists of only of three pages. If one considers the further musical development of the composition, his "stopping" seems logical. On the one hand, he tends to return to initial thoughts and the material of the main subject, while on the

components Arnold outlined, b) to what extent these were developed, and c) which elements are not mentioned in the sketches at all and which must have been added later, during the process of orchestration. We might therefore assume that they belonged to Arnold's normative vocabulary and represent his individual style.

An initial look at the first sketch sheet reveals that Arnold outlines substantially more than usual. Notes on instrumentation, such as the singular words "brass" and "percussion", as well as individual instruments like "oboe" or "tuba", are clearly indicated. The dynamic is precisely outlined by several markings, and the piano short score is comprised of, according to the required space for outlining, two to four systems. Nevertheless, Arnold's markings next to the rehearsal letters C and F reveal special charm. These markings, referring to the first and second subjects, give an explanation about Arnold's clear classicism and distinctive form. After a short introductory part, the overture stringently follows more or less a sonata form, although the harmonic dualism between the tonic and the dominant, being so essential for the entire classical period,[37] does not play an important role.

Comparing the first five bars of the piano short sketch of the *Robert Kett Overture* to the later version for full orchestra, one might conclude that Arnold's process of orchestration is apparently more "copy-work" than creative art. He "obeys" his own allocations (see "brass" mentioned in the short score), and the opening trumpets notated in the lower system of the short score are answered by fugato-like trombones. Nevertheless, Arnold minimally deviates from predetermined "rules" from the sketch. In the full score, he modifies the octave register of the trombones and notates them an octave higher than in the short score. This can be explained by the fact that the sound effect of these extremely low trombones would have been very unsatisfactory.[38]

The full score will now be analysed in greater depth.

At letter A, we are confronted with an Alla Marcia section, its rhythm assigned to the tenor drum within the percussion section of the full

---

other hand, he finally increases the tension of the overture by writing out a C-major chord battle in the finale of the composition. This battle cannot avoid comparison in its absurdity to *A Grand, Grand Festival Overture, opus 57*, which was composed in 1956.

[37] In this context *cf.* Rosens's statements on the polarity between tonic and dominant as well as on the sonata form (ROSEN 1997: 23ff;30ff)

[38] The word "Introduction" marked in the short score is missing in the later full score.

score, though this allocation must be deducted from Arnold's marking in the short score at letter B. The following four bars are fascinating in terms of what Arnold had outlined in the sketch compared with what he later added to the full score. A sustained A-minor seventh chord, later turning by means of slur notes into a G-major seventh chord, can be found in the horns (one bar after A). However, this process, at first seemingly quite simple, is framed by orchestral effects of great ingenuity. Arnold, applying a glissando effect to the strings, "slides" from one chord to another. As a result, a new harmonic context is created, established by a new bass line not expressed in the short score (the notes C and G as well as F and G in the tuba, timpani, and pizzicato contrabasses), and the passage, at first apparently quite simple, evokes a substantially more advanced compositional impression.

The following bars from letter B onward roughly correspond to the outlined structure in the short score, although they cannot be described as thematic substance. The entry of the first subject in the piccolo flute, combined with timpani and low violoncellos "beating" vague strokes on C, does not differ from the short score. However, it is surprising that Arnold did not transfer the E-fortepiano octaves of the horns (one bar before letter D) to the full score at all, although the appearance of this "swelling effect" could have been quite recognisable. Arnold substituted this element in the full score through the use of various unison octaves of B flat and D; the unisons as a stylistic element are often applied by Arnold. It is not evident why Arnold renounced these fortepiano elements at the beginning (cf. the swelling of the fortepiano chord before A).

Analysing the beginning of page 2 of the short score, one notices a bar that has been completely scribbled out. However, in comparison to the previous page, it becomes obvious that this must have been a slip of Arnold's pen.

If one now pursues the following development of the short score and compares it to the full orchestral score, it becomes evident that they correspond to each other in almost every detail. They differ neither in choice of octave range nor in selection of instrument positions. However, two bars before I, Arnold surprisingly chooses to modify the outlined C-major chord in the root position (short score) to the first inversion (full score). The sound mixture of low strings, trombones, horns, and bassoons, as well as clarinets in their Chalumeau Register in this location, is innovative and creates an excellent overall impression in terms of sound and timbre.

The *Overture Robert Kett* evokes an almost irrational image with its orchestral and compositional development. Apart from the divergences already described, Arnold's orchestration creates the notion of an unfinished jigsaw puzzle. The marginal mixture of different instrumental bodies is confusing, the sound produced is generally coupled with a single instrumental body (brass, woodwindss, strings), and, within the tutti sections, the scoring of unisons and doublings predominate. One misses the early Arnold, carefully devoted to the smallest details and able to create brilliantly scored orchestral fireworks, a master of colourful orchestration. Remembering the overwhelming impression of both sets of the *English Dances*, it **seems** that Arnold had lost control of his orchestration skills. Nevertheless, Arnold's late works – especially his 9th Symphony, which will be discussed later – have their own special charm. Arnold's charm focuses on the essentials of composition: the tone, the sound, or special outstanding orchestral effects (e.g., the glissando in the strings). Arnold's magic, which had long been derided by critics, had made him popular with audiences, had changed. Instead of concentrating on orchestral colours, the tones and their qualities in and of themselves became predominant in their importance.

What are the essentials of Arnold's composition process? First, they need to be considered in relative terms, as we cannot form a complete picture of a composer by analysing only two works. However, focusing on a single quintessential point has turned out to be useful. Jackson's image of Arnold as a non-sketching composer (JACKSON 2003:13) must be regarded as incorrect. On the other hand, by analysing Arnold's composition process in depth and separating it into steps, it is possible to show Arnold's actual daily struggle as a composer.

One might argue that Arnold's use of short scores was influenced by the simple structure in both works described, which use a relatively linear structure (usually melody as the main element, a chord layer, an accompaniment layer, and,rarely, the use of counterpoint). However, such a conclusion would be incorrect. The autograph of an early piano work by Arnold, *The Dream City*, composed in 1938, shows that Arnold regularly tried out possible orchestrations by simply writing annotations them onto his short scores.

Figure 8 *The Dream City* for solo piano (1938)

(Reproduced by kind permission of the Arnold Estate.)

The reason for the pertinacious postulation within Arnoldian circles that **no** short scores by Arnold existed may be grounded in the idea that contemporary composers often aesthetically preferred to tell the public that a composition could be generated without the use of an instrument. The trace of the "unaesthetic" – "Is there anybody still writing music at the **piano**?" –obscured an unbiased view of Arnold's works. But, can quality be validated only through a belief in the "genius myth"?

The fact that Arnold rarely scribbled or corrected might have something to do with his practical approach to writing music: "...Writing music, that is, the actual physical job of getting it on paper, I consider as donkey-work. When a single chord which takes a second to perform can

44

take one half-hour to write out, it is much better to keep writing new ones than to bother making minor alterations on old ones..." (SCHAFER 1963:152)

To write something down and be completely persuaded of it should be regarded as a quality. Instead, Arnold was often faced with the argument that his style was arbitrary. Arnold was much more profound than many commentators intended to make others believe, even if he did not write music in the style of the highly sophisticated avant-garde of the 1950s and 1960s. He did not compose in an unreflective way at all. Arnold's aspiration to achieve unity and form[39] had its origins in his compositional models: Berlioz, Mahler, and Sibelius.

It shall become clear in the course of this study whether he fulfilled the high demands he placed on himself.

---

[39] cf. Arnold's own statements in his essay, "I Think Of Music In Terms Of Sounds", first published in *Music and Musicians*, July 1956, reprinted in Burton-Page's "Philharmonic Concerto" (ARNOLD 1956:168f).

Figure 9 *Robert Kett Overture*, original sketch, page 1

(Reproduced by kind permission of the Arnold Estate.)
Robert Kett Overture, op. 141
Music by Malcolm Arnold
© Copyright 1990 Novello & Company Limited
All Rights Reserved. International Copyright Secured.
Reproduced by Permission

Figure 10 *Robert Kett Overture*, original sketch, page 2

Figure 11 *Robert Kett Overture*, original sketch, page 3

2. The Myth of Invention: A Case Study on Arnold's Composition Process and Orchestration Technique

2. The Myth of Invention: A Case Study on Arnold's Composition Process and Orchestration Technique

3. Understanding the Concept of "Tradition" and Early Symphonic Writing: From Mahlerian Scenery to Arnold's Independence from Sibelius

*"...The hero is dead, the symphony should be over –
but there are still some 400 bars to go..." Daniel K. L. Chua
(CHUA 1999:157)*

3.1 Understanding the Concept of "Tradition"

Classifying a composer by placing him in a single category is enticing; once established, such a classification is easy to fall back on but is almost impossible to refute.

If a classification is believed to define some core attribute, it is not easy for a person to free himself of that label. And if he does, no flavour remains. Labels cannot be escaped – or can they?

What is common to most of these classifications is a dependence on the concepts of "tradition" and "convention" – the latter also often tied to a "stereotype", easily leading to negative connotations. The conventional or conservative Arnold, Arnold the traditionalist, Arnold the symphonist, or – pejoratively – the reactionary Arnold, encompasses many of these attributes, and even when only the positive are focused on,[40] the following is clear. In order to properly analyse the Arnold phenomenon, one must understand the roots of these classifications. If Arnold's traditions and models are to be correctly understood, they must be investigated, enabling us to properly position him and his work.

Thus we shall now approach the theoretical concept of tradition, using Lissa's (1973), Eggebrecht's (1973), and Hobsbawn's (2003) definitions as examples. Further, Arnold's two most striking early works, the *English Dances, Set I, opus 27* (1950) and *Set II, opus 33* (1951) and his *2nd Symphony*, opus 40 (1953) are discussed within an analytical context for three reasons. First, Arnold himself has emphasised the importance of composers as models as well as their masterly control of compositional technique. In several written statements he names Sibelius and Mahler as masters (ARNOLD 1956:168; SCHAFER 1963:151).

Second, this influence can be worked out in particular with a composition-analytical view. It shall be precisely indicated, and illustrated by precise extracts, which influences were taken from Mahler and Sibelius and which components were original, or "Arnoldish". The extent to which Arnold had already developed his own personal style in this early period

---

[40] Whittall considers him the "British successor" of Vaughan Williams (WHITTALL 1999:68), calling him a "practitioner" of the symphony (WHITTALL 1999:349); Morrin, however, describes Arnold's style as follows: "Much of it is light in nature" (MORRIN 2002:14).

will be revealed, and it will be clearly shown that he was more than an imitator.[41] The roles of stereotype and convention – in Arnold's eyes as well as in the eyes of recipients – will also be discussed.

Third, both sets of the *English Dances* are particularly omnipresent in Great Britain, so we must look at the connotations of "Englishness" displayed in them. *What the Papers Say*, the longest running news programme on the BBC and broadcast for the first time on 5 November, 1956, has used the fifth movement of the sets, *Allegro Non Troppo*, as its theme music since 1969. To quote Oscar H. Schmitz, Arnold as a *Gassenhauer*?

Finally, the diametrically opposed positions of two important figures in British musical life (BBC music journalist Hans Keller, who rejected Arnold's music, and Donald Mitchell, who truly acknowledged it) shall be discussed and qualified from today's perspective.

Zofia Lissa has chosen a very informative point of view. Instead of operating within the relatively wide concept of tradition, she limits herself to purely musical phenomena. She introduces the concept of the „musikalischen Geschichtsbewusstsein" *"consciousness of music history"* and describes this as: „...Informationsfeld klanglicher Natur, das in der Fühlungnahme mit der Musik verschiedener Jahrhunderte, Epochen und Stile gewonnen wird. Dieses bewirkt in uns vielerlei Stereotype der musikalischen Vorstellung, die für jeden dieser Kodes etwas anders geartet sind; ferner unterschiedliche rezeptive Haltungen, die später beim verschiedenen Material eingenommen werden; der Begriff des musikalischen Geschichtsbewusstseins umfasst auch das Gefühl der Zugehörigkeit zu einem der vielartigen Evolutionskontinua als der eigenen kulturellen Tradition. Darüber hinaus umfasst es auch das Gefühl der Kontinuität der Stile, d.h. die Vorstellung von ihren Ähnlichkeiten und Unterschieden und dem daraus folgenden Wissen über ihre genetischen oder auch nur chronologischen Verknüpfungen..." (LISSA 1973:11) *"...a field of information of a tonal [sound] nature which is won by the empathy within the music of different centuries, epochs and styles. This creates in us various clichés of musical images that are different for each of these codes; it further creates different receptive postures we must cope with within different materials; the concept of the consciousness of music history also encompasses the knowledge of the affiliation to one of the various evolutionary continua, as their own cultural tradition. In addition, it also encloses the feeling of the continuity of the styles, i.e., the image of their resemblances and differences and the resulting knowledge about their genesis or even chronological linkings..."*

What is so striking about Lissa's approach is the fact that, as soon as we perceive something that apparently belongs to tradition and to a

---

[41] Since: "...Wer nur durch historische Anleihen seinen Stil findet und auf Stilnachahmung angewiesen ist, verrät seine schöpferische Schwäche und geistige Impotenz...Zu blutleerer Scholastik führt solch nostalgischer Historismus allemal: nicht nur in der Theologie, auch in der Kunst..." (KÜNG 2006:223). *"...Who finds his style only by historical loans and is dependent on style imitation betrays his creative weakness and spiritual impotence...Bloodless scholasticism always leads to such nostalgic historicism: not only in theology, also in the arts..."*

certain musical consciousness, we are no longer free from immediately predetermined associations. Our attitudes are pre-programmed in a certain way; even if we approach, without prejudice, a musical work that is unknown to us, we have expectations and often evaluate divergences as inhomogeneous. The ability to have a feeling for style or to adequately recognise styles is much more important in categorising single composers than has been stated before. The role of the composer and his self-image also cannot be forgotten. We must discuss whether, and to what extent, Arnold was aware of his own consciousness of music history and whether he considered the current expectations of his listeners as less or more important than his own.

Eggebrecht's approach in the same collection of articles is distinguished by two prongs. He defines the concept of tradition, not substituting it as Lissa does, but instead dividing it into two sub-groups: the „waltenden" *(the "prevailing")* tradition and the „begriffenen" *(the "understood")* tradition (EGGEBRECHT 1973:54). While the first concept means the unconscious rule by tradition, therefore referring to the unreflektierten Gewohnheiten des Sich-Verhaltens und Handelns *("unreflected customs of one's own behaviour and action"),* the understood tradition explicitly discovers and, as a consequence, is itself also uncovered.

He also focuses on the concept of historical consciousness, even more strongly than Lissa does, as an aesthetic and demanding component. The purpose of a pure discussion of the consciousness of music history, according to Eggebrecht, must be: „dass man [sich] nicht [nur] in der Geschichte weiß... Geschichtsbewusstsein heißt, dass man, sich in der Geschichte wissend, die Geschichte wissen will, um die Stereotypen zu durchschauen, die das Bewusstsein - unbewusst - determinieren d.h. um den Freiheitsraum zu finden und zu vergrößern, in dem das Ich im Erfassen und Begreifen der gegenwärtigen Wirklichkeit die Entscheidungen trifft über das Abwerfen und Annehmen seiner Determination, das Verwerfen und Akzeptieren von Traditionsprozessen und objekten, und somit die Geschichte, in der es sich weiß, beherrschen lernt..." (EGGEBRECHT 1973:63) *"that one does not only know himself inside history...Historical consciousness means that we, being inside history, want to know history in order to see through the clichés, determining the consciousness - unconsciously - i.e., in order to find and to increase the space of freedom in which the 'self', by perceiving and understanding the present reality, makes decisions about rejecting and accepting this determination, rejecting and accepting traditional processes and traditional objects, and therefore learning to control the history in which it knows itself...".*

Eggebrecht's claim is much more absolute and is tied together much more strongly with a possible judgement about the value of an artistic product. An artist who does not strive to know himself "inside history" and who does not try to get to know the degree of closeness between stereotypes and his own freedom risks his piece of art being perceived as not a true piece of art but as an imitation, a pastiche. Indeed, Eggebrecht does not propagate the characteristic style of an instruction as Adorno does – Adorno's choice of words „Wahrheit" *("truth")* or „Die Schäbigkeit und Vernutztheit des verminderten Septimakkords" *("the shabbiness and tiredness of the diminished seventh chord")[42]* clearly underscores this. Nevertheless, Eggebrecht's virtuoso-controlled deposition of causal logic is not far from imposing explicit aesthetic requirements for a piece of art.

Although Eric Hobsbawm is not a member of the musicological discipline but operates instead as a historian, his closeness to Eggebrecht's model is striking. He speaks of the "invented tradition" and marks this practise by the fact that behaviour patterns of normative character, characterised by repetitive emergent application, immediately create past relations to and therefore continuity with the past (HOBSBAWM 2003:1). Tradition would be "invented" by the fact that processes could be formalised by the society involved and would at the same time be ritualised – presumably, there is a backward relationship with the past: "...Inventing traditions...is essentially a process of formalisation and ritualisation, characterized by reference to the past, if only by imposing repetition..." (HOBSBAWM 2003:4).

He suggests, analogously to Eggebrecht, a division of the concept of tradition into two categories. First, tradition should be seen as clearly separated from custom. Indeed, in the latter, innovation would not be excluded in terms of progress. However: "...'Custom' in traditional societies has the double function of motor and fly-wheel. It does not preclude innovation and change up to a point, though evidently the requirement that it must appear compatible or even identical with precedent imposes substantial limitations on it. What it does is to give any desired change (or resistance to

---

[42] Indeed, Adorno's statements in his *Philosophy of New Music* (1947) on artistic freedom must be viewed in relative terms against the background of the special aesthetic position of contemporary music in Germany around 1950.Today, Adorno's sharp statements sound somewhat strange, however; "...By no means do all tonal combinations ever employed stand indifferently at the disposal of the composer today. Even the duller ear perceives the shabbiness and tiredness of the diminished seventh chord or of certain chromatic passing notes in the salon music of the nineteenth century. For the technically experiienced ear, vague discontent of this kind is transformed into a canon of prohibitions. If all is not deception, this canon now debars the means of tonality, which is to say, the whole of traditional music. Not only are these sounds obsolete und unfashionable. They are false. They no longer fullfill their function. The most advanced level of technical procedures prescribes task compared to which the traditional sounds prove to be powerless clichés. There are modern compositions that occasionally intersperse tonal sounds in their own nexus. In these instances it is the triads that are cacophonous, not the dissonances. At proxy for the dissonances these triads may sometimes be justified. But it is not merely the stylistic impurity that is responsible for their falsity. Rather, today, the technical horizon against which the tonal sounds detestably obtrude encompasses the whole of music. When a contemporary composer, just as Jean Sibelius, makes do entirely with tonal resourcs, they sound just as false as do the tonal enclaves in atonal music. Admittedly, reservations are required here. What is decisive in the truth and falsity of chords is not their isolated occurrence. It is measurable exclusively by the total level of technique..." (ADORNO 2006:32-33).

innovation) the sanction of precedent, social continuity and natural law as expressed in history..." (HOBSBAWM 2003:2).

Hobsbawm further distinguishes "invented tradition" from "routine" or "convention", all of which create new methods within the scope of social networks by means of constant repetition. Nevertheless, they deal with pure functional processes and, above all, with their inability to found new ideological movements or to serve as a basis for them.

In Frederick Loewe's world-renowned musical My Fair Lady, based on George Bernard Shaw's Pygmalion, the protagonist, Professor Higgins, complains about the horrible London accents whose sound shifts prevent understanding of spoken language. He questions this in the following lines:

"Why can't the English teach their children how to speak?

This verbal class distinction by now should be antique.

If you spoke as she does, Sir, instead of the way you do,

Why, you might be selling flowers too... (Pickering: I beg your pardon!)

An Englishman's way of speaking absolutely classifies him.

The moment he talks he makes some other Englishman despise him.

One common language I'm afraid we'll never get.

Oh, why can't the English learn to set a good example for people

Whose English is painful to your ears..." (LOEWE 1969: 18-20).

Even if we do not grant this text much academic credibility, the point is clear. Higgins vividly describes a possible self-image of a British man of a certain class defining his identity based on his speech.

A compositional identity is in this connection not too different from Higgins's image of accents as a means of class differentiation. Thus, one composer can be differentiated from another simply by his choice of compositional means, his "manner of speech". The general perception and classification of a work should still not be limited only to its musical parameters. On the contrary, external musical contexts, the purpose of a performance, and the intended audience must all be discussed.

Hubert Parry chose a typical title for his suite-like compositions for string orchestra, An English[43] Suite. It consists of seven short movements. Let us look at the musical composition itself. Can we regard it as genuinely "English"?

The Prelude begins vitally with a tutti G-major texture. Its baroque gesture is underscored by the use of a fundamental bass (throughout bass) and canonic imitation.[44] The texture is homogeneous, almost "thick", and the harmonic development, except in letter C, is not striking, usually referring to the initial tonic G major. Also, the Minuet that follows is hardly different in harmonic terms; also in G major, it does not surprise the listener. As in the Prelude, semiquaver figures are alternated with quavers, supported by the fundamental bass in crotchets or quavers. From a harmonic perspective, the third movement, the Saraband, can be described as probably the most intense movement. The Caprice recreates Mendelssohn's spirit; we

---

[43] Saremba points out that the „....unter Leitung des Komponisten uraufgeführte 3. Symphonie [1889] in C-Dur, die den Beinamen *The English*, trägt, als die populärste..." (SAREMBA 1994:72) (*"...3rd Symphony in C major, often also labelled as "The English", first premiered under the direction of the composer, is considered the most popular..."* of Parry's five symphonies.

[44] The fact that the title "Suite" comes from the baroque epoch will not to be focused on.

can speculate that Parry felt close to Mendelssohn because of the time he spent studying in Germany. The fact that Parry further imitated baroque styles can be traced back to his music-analytical interest in Bach: in 1909, his treatise, *Johann Sebastian Bach: The Story of the Development of a Great Personality*, was published.

Although the analytic remarks here are consciously brief, we can still recognise one prominent feature. Parry composed a work whose musical effect – partially due to the quoted pseudo-Baroque gesture – is a mediation of dignity and pride, but in harmonic terms he created a "toothless" work. To call this work "English" can hardly be argued; Parry neither uses any significant contributions from English Renaissance music, nor, in this case, does he use any elements of English folk music. Parry's approach to *An English Suite* is perhaps even comparable to Brahms's approach to his Hungarian Dances. The difference is that Brahms, as a non-Hungarian, perceives a sort of Hungarian music, melding it with his personal style and therefore still producing a typical piece of "Brahms". Parry presumably chose the title of the suite to make a contribution as a composer to the pride of the nation. Even if we believe Saremba's statement that Parry was linked to the *Ranküne* of the upper classes and faced the dogmatism of the church (SAREMBA 1994:66), as the director of the Royal College of Music in London he represented in particular this "Englishness."

Here the circle of discussion may be closed and we return to the initial object of research, Arnold's compositional style. Where Arnold substantially uses current topoi, we must question whether this is "tradition" in the above-mentioned sense or whether he sticks to pure convention or the use of stereotypes – the latter always creating a danger of displaying artistic emptiness. Regarding the *English Dances*, one can ask provocatively: What are the generic, original "English" elements from which the dances earn their title? Where does Arnold return to conventional forms and topoi? What can be regarded as a cliché, and where do we find Arnold's own compositional personality that will allow Arnold himself to become a stylistic model for the following generation, a creator of "invented tradition" in Hobsbawm's sense? The following thoughts on Arnold's *English Dances* aim to answer these questions.

3.2 Early Symphonic Writing and Mahler

Arnold's *English Dances* were composed in 1950/1951 with the explicit permission of his publisher, Bernard de Nevers (Legnick). Nevers asked composers affiliated with his publishing house, including Arnold and Franz Reizenstein, to compose a comparable popular orchestral work in the style of Dvorak's *Slavonic Dances*. This request was not fulfilled and did not lead to the expected result – except for Arnold sending him, instead of a single composition, an entire set of four dances in December 1950 (COLE 1989:38; BURTON-PAGE 1994:59-60; JACKSON 2003:58-59; HARRIS/MEREDITH 2004:113). The work, later supplemented by another set of four dances, was a big commercial success for both publisher and composer and emerged as one of the works that inspired various generations growing up in Great Britain.

If we intend to ask (as we did regarding Parry's *An English Suite*) why they are labelled "English" and to what extent that characterisation is accurate, we must provide a logical interpretation in Arnold's case, as well. Bearing in mind the genesis of the composition – it was composed as a commercial work to complement a publisher's catalogue – one might tend to think that the label was only used for this reason. However, Arnold's compositional fracture is different from Parry's *An English Suite*, the latter creating the notion of a tasteless Bach pastiche because of its harmonic language being reduced almost to the diatonic. Arnold's musical language is, in contrast, independent, sophisticated, and rich in its orchestral colours as well as in its expressiveness. At the very beginning of the first movement, Arnold confronts us with a typical sign of his style: he first sets up a harmonic ostinato in the form of two parallel sustained seventh chords (D-major with a major seventh, E-minor seventh chord), tied together with an equally ostinato bass foundation, before building on this one melody based on the D-major scale (violins).

It is conceived in a dreamy gesture; its limited tonal material equalises with skillful rotary figures and wakes – as opposed to Parry – immediately associating it with Irish folk music and fiddle tunes.

Until letter D Arnold limits himself exclusively to the principal subject, and develops from A the supplemental contrapuntal colouring in the woodwindss until, in B and C, the woodwinds state the subject in unison octaves. In D, a short intermezzo is introduced, in which the parallel, now-descending seventh chords establish a harmonic setting in the brasses, flanked by non-thematic single contrapuntal lines in different instruments (horns, oboes, and flutes). A colour contrast is developed between the sonorous brass section and the substantially brighter woodwinds. The musical form of the first movement (andantino) can be described as a simple A-B-A form.

Figure 12 *English Dances, Set I, opus 27,* 1st **movement (excerpt)**

Reproduced by permission Alfred Lengnick & Co Ltd.

What makes the *English Dances* one of Arnold's early core works, and what is its compositional quality?

It is not only his excellent orchestration technique – for instance the ingeniously roguish instrumentation of the second movement in which strikingly grace notes are varied in infinite combinations. Arnold also knows how to create gigantic orchestral tutti fireworks. Arnold differentiates convention from tradition in a very personal way; he is not their victim and does not compose a modelled folk dance like Dvorak's *Slavonic Dances*. Umberto Eco, although from a linguistic perspective, refers to the convention of rhymes, stating that a bestselling lyricist would often act reflexively, rhyming "Herz" with "Schmerz"[45] (ECO 1973:259-260). In contrast, Arnold composes carefully and intuitively, but not reflexively. The fifth movement from *Set II*, with its military characteristics, could easily have become a Bohemian polka. However, Arnold prevented this by neutralising the principal subject with an easy but effective trick. He produced a counterpole to the tin whistle-like solo piccolo subject. The strings always stress the tonic-dominant relationship at the end of the eight-bar subject with gruff fortissimo marked quavers (*cf.* one bar before A).

---

[45] A German pun: "heart" and "pain" almost sound the same.

Figure 13 *English Dances, Set II, opus 33*, **fifth movement (excerpt)**

Reproduced by permission Alfred Lengnick & Co Ltd.

The degree of tension and movement between the fifth and first scale, worked out by means of a *resolutio quartae*, is established through further development and becomes style-immanent. It appears in very different constellations, in a solo as well as in a chordic tutti orchestration (literal or even modified to a harmonic structure, *cf.* one before D), but is then turned around and functionally used almost ad absurdum (three bars before C, one bar before K). The function of marking the tonic-dominant relationship is abandonded, but for Arnold, it creates the possibility to head towards the most disparate tonal regions: C minor (letter B), A major (letter F, notice the tritone constellation to the actual main tonality of E-flat major). One might argue that these procedures are conventional and stereotypical. But, as simple as the means are, in the context of the composition it becomes obvious that Arnold opposes their conventional application by making them unfamiliar; therefore, by composing the *English Dances*, he contributes a piece of art rather than a stereotypical dance.[46]

Arnold's 2nd Symphony, opus 40 (1953) has remained in his contemporary adaptation and to this day is a symphonic work that inspires fascination as well as aversion. Its premiere was a weighty experience in the history of British musical life, underscored by the attention paid to it by a variety of annotators in professional journals (*Musical Opinion, Musical Review, The Music Review*). Indeed, it is worth critically examining the perceptions expressed at that time.

Apart from the support of the journal *Musical Opinion* (1953), "...Of all our younger composers I regard Malcolm Arnold as the most promising. He has immense technical power, and a facility which rarely leads him astray, and usually gives his music a fluency... Thank God, at last here is some sane, healthy, invigorating music, written by a composer who has ideas, technique and a melodic gift! Let us hope the Symphony has the success it richly deserves - British music will be all the better for that..." (ANON. 1953:611), the criticism of the music journalists and musicologists Hans Keller and Donald Mitchell, with their diametrically opposed positions, shall be discussed next.[47]

In the glossy *The New in Review*, Keller refers first to two of Arnold's works, the *John Clare Cantata, opus 52*, and the *Piano Trio, opus 54*, describing them as disappointing and stating that they were "weak works disclosing insufficient self-control" (KELLER 1956:333).

---

[46] *cf.* in this connection Goldmann's statement: „....Wichtig ist, dass die Klischees ihrerseits durch den Kontext verändert werden, wenn möglich so, dass sie ihre Klischeehaftigkeit, nicht notwendig ihre Geschichtlichkeit, verlieren. Funktionieren kann das - wenn überhaupt - nur, sofern es gelingt, den neuen Kontext eigenständig zu gestalten, ob nun rational organisiert oder wie immer sonst. Simple Wideraufnahme von Klischees im klischeehaften Kontext, womöglich als neue Unmittelbarkeit sich verstehend oder auch bloß verspielt danach schielend, kann kaum zu etwas anderem führen als zur Verstärkung der allgemeinen Expansion von Klischeebildung..." (GOLDMANN 1994:32-33). (*"...It is important that stereotypes are changed by their context, if possible in such a way that they lose their clicheness, not inevitably their history. This can only work - generally - provided that one succeeds in independently forming the new context, whether now organised rationally or, as usual, otherwise. Simple recollection of stereotypes in the stereotyped context, maybe even understanding this as a new direction, can hardly lead to something other than the strengthening of the general expansion of stereotypes..."*)

[47] *cf.* in this context Redlich's statement, although it reveals his tendency to describe Arnold as mainly a composer of film music: *"Arnold's obsession with unaltered thematic quotation...may be a reaction of his subconscious to the primitive Leitmotif technique often required by the film. The poster-like blatancy of the finale...may also be traced back to the questionable habits of film composers..."* (REDLICH 1955:163).

However, what is surprising (bearing in mind Keller's highly qualified music-analytical descriptions of Mozart and Britten[48]) is the intensity he, with incomprehensible meticulousness, devotes to a putative problem of Arnold's orchestration, reserving 39 lines for this description. Keller first criticises Arnold as "one of the most skillful orchestrators now living" and uses as a counterargument Arnold's use of the fortepiano horns and oboes/clarinets in the scherzo at letter D. He argues that they would be completely covered by the preceding fortissimi. His argument is as follows: "...This is the kind of mistake which orchestral player-composers [Arnold had been described as a composer and trumpet player] are in fact particularly liable to make, because things sound different from their positions, and a *subito piano* in particular is more readily perceived within the playing body. In order to make quite sure that my critical reaction was not partly determined by the acoustics of the Albert Hall, I borrowed the record of, again, Arnold's own performance, and found my impression (which indeed can be formed on the basis of the score alone) confirmed...The problem has of course always existed and often depends on the performer's and conductor's understanding co-operation for its solution, even in supremely orchestrated scores...In the Arnold...there is no preparation, nor is there any chance for the conductor to do anything, since the structure is continuous in either instance..." (KELLER 1956:333). Keller's final interpretation is predetermined here, unfortunately, by his first impression, and the possibility that the insufficient use of microphones[49] could perhaps have created this impression is not considered at all. As simplistic as it may sound, Keller succumbs in a certain way to the reviewer's illness (Goethe's reviewers's illness) in his pre-cast opinion of Arnold's orchestration: "...there is no doubt that...Arnold is a natural orchestrator, but to call him at this stage...'one of the most skilful orchestrators now living' is tosh: skill is in fact one of the few accomplishments which his orchestration sometimes lacks..." (KELLER 1956:33). His quite peculiar viewpoint cannot be justified by his argument.

Arnold's orchestration shows, in comparison to his compositional models (I will later discuss the Mahler component in more depth) an astonishing transparency. There is no large contrapuntal weaving as (for instance) in Mahler's 1st Symphony. Instead, Arnold concentrates on the clear presentment of musical ideas – an impression that is supported at first glance by the score layout with its pausing instruments. Contrapuntal ideas are sporadically developed as the canonical entry of the woodwinds in relation to the brass section (woodwinds, trumpets, and trombones *cf.* bar 123 et seqq.). As a rule, the instrumental bodies complement each other, often also in a quizzical way (*cf.* the second movement, with its contrast between the woodwinds and the pizz strings) without overlapping one another. And, if Arnold wants to underline this transparency, as in the first

---

[48] *cf.* the extensive Keller articles, recently published by Christopher Wintle (WINTLE 2005), as well as Keller's so-called "Functional Analysis", which is still prominent in Great Britain (KELLER 2001).

[49] The Arnold recording Keller refers to is a mono recording (!) and has only recently been remastered.

movement from letter $\boxed{O}$ onward, he surprises the listener with a sudden reduced two-part texture (cf. $\boxed{P}$). Significant tutti-scoring, which Sibelius often preferred, is rather a rarity, except for the final situation in the second movement at $\boxed{R}$. Keller has overemphasised a single observation and has therefore become the victim of his preconception; he has not perceived and therefore not appreciated Arnold's masterly shadings and contrasts in orchestration.

Keller also describes a second problem with the 2nd Symphony, which can be regarded as a coda problem: "[it]...is the structural function of the concluding section in the profoundly original sonata form that is the first movement" (KELLER 1956:334). He argues that in tonal music, the coda is usually based on the material of the first subject, supporting the main key (tonic) by the tonic itself or by means of a modulation. He postulates that Arnold's final bars could therefore not be regarded as a coda: "...Now our so-called "coda" is stably in A major, the key of the second subject and the one furthest removed from the tonic (E flat); it evinces neither a modulatory confirmation of the tonic nor principal thematicism. The truth is that Arnold is here able to introduce what, harmonically, amounts to a second second-subject stage, owing to the facts (a) that there is a great [deal] of tonic confirmation throughout the movement which returns to E flat before the development, and (b) that the development is itself tonally stable...as opposed to developmental modulations. In the thoroughly tonical recapitulation, the second subject is enclosed between two statements of the first, the *second* of which corresponds to the *first* of the three tonic statements of this main theme in the exposition. The only essential thing, then, that is still 'missing' after the recapitulation of the first subject's first statement is the material of the bridge passage, which therefore naturally emerges at this second harmonic second-subject stage. The real coda is quite short (4 bars) and founded, conventionally after this unconventional excursion, on the basic motifs, which thus gives its final confirmation of the basic key..." (KELLER 1956:334).

Even Keller limits his argument by stating that his criticism did not have anything in common with a "pedantic classification"[50] (KELLER 1956:335). A comparison with the full score reveals that Keller's opinion must be seen in relative terms. His argument is questionable in at least two respects: philosophically-aesthetically and compositionally.

The origins of Keller's position are clear from the outset. When Arnold, more or less unambiguously, chooses the form of a sonata for the first movement of the 2nd Symphony, he acts conventionally and normatively; this normative choice, used in countless symphonies by Arnold's predecessors, creates a certain expectation. Keller, who is completely competent in his knowledge and awareness of the historical development of the sonata, forgets in his argument that compositional freedom means being free to choose one's means, free to be unconventional– something that Keller had criticised. Indeed, it is unquestionable that Arnold uses this classical form and that his

---

[50] In the same paragraph, though, he makes a rather unflattering comparison between Arnold's word with Tchaikovsky's symphonic music (KELLER 1956:335).

63

interpretation, dividing the movements roughly into exposition-development-recapitulation with the coda, is correct. But Keller's approach of assessing Arnold aesthetically in terms of "true" and "false" is reminiscent of the difficulty with which many music theorists and musicologists faced the phenomenon of Schubert. Arnold had hardly been influenced by Schubert – this can be easily proved – and his vocal works are clearly different from Schubert's *Lieder*. However, it is interesting in this connection to examine Charles Rosen's statements on Schubert's style break and to review them in the context of Keller's analysis: "The synthesis of the means of expression we call the classical style was by no means exhausted when it was abandoned, but submission to ist discipline was not an easy matter...Schubert, however, cannot be easily placed into any one category – Romantic, post-classical, or classical – and he stands as an example of the resistance of the material of history to the most necessary generalizations, and as a reminder of the irreducibly personal facts that underlie the history of style...

A style, when it is no longer the natural mode of expressions, gains a new life – a shadowy life-in-death – as a prolongation of the past. We imagine ourselves able to revive the past through its art, to perpetuate it by continuing to work within its conventions. For this illusion of reliving history, the style must be prevented from becoming truly alive once again. The conventions must remain conventional, the forms lose their orginal significance in order to take on their new responsibility of evoking the past...The true inheritors of the classical style were not those who maintained ist traditions, but those, from Chopin to Debussy, who preserved ist freedom as they gradually altered and finally destroyed the musical language which had made the creation of the style possible..." (ROSEN 1997:522).

Comparing Keller's and Rosen's music-theoretical and style-aesthetic statements from a historical viewpoint is problematic – music theory underwent major paradigmatic changes after World War II. Still, Arnold cannot be pressed into such a restraining corset. It is, though, equally unlikely that Arnold generally undertook such aesthetic considerations of art on his own. He used the form as a costume, even a uniform, without regulating himself, becoming an innovator and heir in Rosen's sense.[51]

---

[51] Moseler's description of Arnold's personal style is likewise informative: „...Die formalen Gegebenheiten werden mit hoher instrumentaler Virtuosität und satztechnischer Professionalität bewältigt, und konstituieren einen Personalstil, der seinerseits die Gattung als ‚freie' Form nutzt, deren formaler, sonatensatzmäßiger Ablauf auch ignoriert wird zugunsten eines fantasieartigen thematischen Aufbaus..." (MOSELER 2002:202). (*"...The formal circumstances are mastered with highly instrumental virtuosity and compositional professionalism, and constitute a style which was for him the 'symphony' type as a 'free' form in which a formal, sonata-like setting is also ignored in favour of a fantasia-like thematic construction..."*)

Symphony No. 2, opus 40, Themenübersicht

Malcolm Arnold

Figure 14 *Symphony No. 2, opus 40*: list of subjects, 1ˢᵗ movement

Symphony No. 2, op. 40
Music by Malcolm Arnold
© Copyright 1953 Paterson's Publications Limited.
© Copyright 2004 Novello & Compandy Limited.
All Rights Reserved. International Copyright Secured.
Reproduced by permission.

The compositional component of the work shall now be discussed. If one investigates both subjects of the described works, it is remarkable that they do not depend on each other very strongly for their characteristic style. Both subjects pay tribute to their tonality, the first in E-flat major and the second in A major (notice the tritone constellation) and extensively use a lyrical musical language with many syncopations. The processing technique of both subjects is also not diametrically different. Except for Arnold's transposition of the first subject to C major at letter K, he generally uses both subjects exclusively on their basic harmonic level, i.e., the first theme in E-flat major, and the second in A major. If we concede that Keller understood the symphony with the help of the score, it becomes evident that the issue is not a coda problem but a repetition problem (to which Hans Redlich had already drawn attention in his discussion) (REDLICH 1955:162-163). Let us examine Arnold's approach in a more exact manner. On two opening bars stating a chord of fourths, in bar 3, the first entry of the subject appears in the solo clarinet. From letter A on, the subject is repeated by the strings, softly framed by a chord layer in the woodwinds; in B this layer is moved to the low brass section, while the woodwinds and strings literally state the subject again. At C, a short transition section follows, its function (by taking up the triadic structure of the first subject) being to modulate the key of the second subject to A major. Arnold's important preference for a tritone constellation is not inadvertent.

The development of the second subject follows the basic layout of the first. It first appears in the flutes and oboes in unison and is then directly repeated at $\boxed{E}$, now as a bass line in the violoncelli, the contrabasses, and the contrabassoon; from letter $\boxed{G}$, which can be regarded as the starting point of the development section, Arnold does not quote the first subject but falls back to the harmonic intervallic fourth pattern of the opening bars, elaborating on it further. At letter $\boxed{K}$ (as already mentioned), he states the first subject transposed to the C-major sphere.

In conclusion, we can say that an exclusive consideration from the point of view of the sonata form and its dualism of subjects is counterproductive. Arnold does not want to chisel a piece into a form, but creates an almost pastoral[52] tonal world. He is of the opinion that it is not possible to establish this within the limited frame of the twelve bars of the first subject; therefore, he repeats it over and over in order to elaborate the context. Keller's persistence on the formal aspects of the first movement can be authoritatively justified, but he has not perceived Arnold's attempt to create an overall mood as anything more than a form of scaffolding.

Indeed, Donald Mitchell, editor of numerous musicological journals, does not directly contradict Keller, but summarises his own opinion of Arnold's 2nd Symphony as follows: "...What I have often complained of in Mr. Arnold's earlier works – an impossible disparity in style between the first and second groups in a sonata structure – finds no place in this recent composition; the first movement's singularly unbroken mood, indeed, successfully depends upon thematic groups which smoothly cohere...That Mr. Arnold's music at its best retains its outward clarity of form and texture, while increasing a subtlety of content which becomes ever harder to define, is the most hopeful sign for the future..." (MITCHELL 1954:382)

Mitchell also intensely describes his impression of Mahler's influence as a composer on Arnold: "...Two movements of his symphony [Symphony No. 2], indeed, are exceptionally highly organized - the first and third - and both make subtle demands of the listener while offering equally subtle rewards...The first movement, for instance, seems, on one level, extraordinary naïve; and the impression is made the stronger by the movement's direct relationship to the first movement of Mahler's Fourth (Mr. Arnold's instrumentation, for instance, and the melodic shape and character of the first subject). The influence of Mahler is very strong throughout the whole work; and there is more than a passing likeness between the return of the funeral march in Mahler's Fifth symphony, in the woodwinds and brass alone, with side-drum dominant, and a climactic passage in Mr. Arnold's Lento - a slow march scored for woodwind, brass, and side-drum (prominent), the whole projected over a tonic-dominant ostinato on the

---

[52] The word was not chosen because of the key of E-flat major (!). It is a subjective impression of the author.

timpani (a Mahlerian gesture absent in the model) and soft strokes on the bass drum...

But what is important, and what can surprise, is what a composer does with his eclecticism; and what Mr. Arnold does with his Mahlerian symbols is, as it were, to turn them inside out, so that they assume a new meaning. Hence Mr. Arnold's fascinating first movement, despite its seeming naïvety, relies for its content neither on Mahler's childlike visions nor on his singular brand of ironic naïvety, but offers instead a mood of profound contentment rarely met with in contemporary music. Yet the Mahlerian stylistic affiliations are there and in the slow movement are apt to mislead if one does not catch the new tone of voice..." (MITCHELL 1954:382).

Mitchell's argument is logical in this respect, as is the fact that Mahler's influence on Arnold can be proved by the composer's own statements. But Mitchell's actual observations still need to be examined more closely.

Indeed, the first subject of Arnold's 2nd Symphony is reminiscent of Mahler's 1st Symphony; both share the same melodic contour and the popular tone of the subject is very prominent, particularly since Mahler's subject is based upon his earlier song cycle, *Lieder eines fahrenen Gesellen (Songs of a Travelling Journeyman)*. However, it would be too easy to simply make a general comparison of Arnold's whole 1st Symphony with the thematic structures of Mahler's first movement. Arnold absorbs Mahlerian gestures; however, his composition-processing technique is another story.

Let us now look closely at the third movement of Arnold's 2nd Symphony, already mentioned by Mitchell. There are, above all, two moments that are compositionally noteworthy: first, the eclecticism and the highest dramatic effect combine with musical development that appears insignificantly simple at first glance, and second, the whole formal construction of the movement, which is also simple, but effective. The compositional means that make it striking shall be discussed further.

"Symphony No. 2, opus 40", Thema III. Satz

Malcolm Arnold

Figure 15 *Symphony No. 2, opus 40, 3rd movement, subject*[53]

Symphony No. 2, op. 40
Music by Malcolm Arnold
© Copyright 1953 Paterson's Publications Limited.
© Copyright 2004 Novello & Compandy Limited.
All Rights Reserved. International Copyright Secured.
Reproduced by permission.

Arnold's initial layout of the subject of the 3rd movement can be described, despite its simplicity, as masterful. The degree of dissonance of the melodic voice in connection with the accompanying B-minor third interval rises in correlation to its rhythmic development; in bar 5 the melodic climax of A sharp is reached, defining at the same time the extreme high tone of the ambitus. In bars 6 and 7, the rhythmical development stagnates somewhat, remaining at the same level until the rhythmical values decrease at the end, almost like Renaissance melodic models.

Here, Arnold understands how to maintain tension: while the dissonance is dissolved in the accompanying strings within the last bars by resolving the interval of second into the third, the ascending line C-C sharp-D sharp-F is of major importance, creating an ambiguous effect. The listener, fascinated, waits for the next musical idea to present itself, and his expectations are fulfilled by the viola subject entry in bar 9.

After this, a further entry appears in the oboe, starting at letter B. One tends at first to criticise Arnold's immanent use of episodes rather than developing them as in a full sonata movement. But this perception is incorrect. The context, it turns out, is embellished substantially more than in the first movement; a movement of thirds (sextuplets) in the strings is joined by low chord voicings in the trombones (*cf.* bar 16 et seqq.: B

---

[53] By the author.

68

minor, C major above B, C minor *sixte ajouté* above B natural; E minor). These chords become the constituting element in section C. Arnold creates a polytonality, functionally working as a transitional section to the following subject-entry in the horns (bar 27, one before D). However, the actual effect of this passage, also reminiscent of Messiaen's harmonic language, creates another layer of complexity that becomes immanent from letter E.

3. Understanding the Concept of "Tradition" and Early Symphonic Writing: From Mahlerian Scenery to Arnold's Independence from Sibelius

Figure 16 *Symphony No. 2, opus 40,* **3rd movement, letter** C **to** D

Symphony No. 2, op. 40
Music by Malcolm Arnold
© Copyright 1953 Paterson's Publications Limited.
© Copyright 2004 Novello & Compandy Limited.
All Rights Reserved. International Copyright Secured.
Reproduced by permission.

In E, a contrapuntal structure unobtrusively appears in the piccolo flute. One is inclined to overlook it, not assigning an important function to it in the development of the composition. In a peculiar and almost nerve-wracking way, Arnold systematically reduces the fourth interval of every bar to a third interval, maintaining it at first for a short period of time (b. 36-38), going over to the fourth interval followed by a minor second (F sharp-G) and finally ending on the major third (G flat-B flat).

From then on, Arnold uses this contrapuntal element as a "little something", appearing almost everywhere, sometimes taking over as the main function but also interweaving with other elements as the principal subject (cf. the canonic structure of the subject entry in the low strings, starting in bar 37, beat 3). Now, in a departure from the first movement, in which Arnold often literally "repeated", the repetitive structures are modified in the third movement in a few (but nevertheless important) places. His writing reflects his consciousness; pure schematic "copying" does not take place.

Equally, however, he takes the use of the monothematic subject to the edge of absurdity. Except for the transitional section from letter F to letter K (bar 75), we are confronted over and over with new subject entries; the quaver equals 56 MM. To the mind, this means at least five minutes. Indeed, Arnold's talent for leaving his listeners hanging must be seen in this logical and persistently monothematic substance. Almost as a relief, but still unexpectedly, a dynamic march, whose relationship to Mahler's 5th Symphony has already been mentioned by Mitchell, appears at K. The Mahlerian connotation is thereby evoked through Arnold's arrangement of the percussion section (tam-tam, bells, and bass drum, as well as the tonic-dominant ostinato in the kettledrums) and his use of shrill and aggressively sharply dotted woodwinds and horn fragments of the subject. Although Arnold again returns to the principal subject at L, this time played by the clarinets, the bassoons, and the horns over an already established percussion ostinato, the element of the dotted notes becomes independent beginning at M. The accompanying harmony, sustained in the low brass section, falls back on the harmonic progression already established in B; now at N, Arnold combines these two elements (shrill and sharply dotted woodwinds, percussion ostinato and the accompanying chord progressions) with a renewed subject entry, now extremely prominently scored in the horns **and** trumpets.

Figure 17 *Symphony No. 2, opus 40,* **third movement, letter** K

Symphony No. 2, op. 40
Music by Malcolm Arnold
© Copyright 1953 Paterson's Publications Limited.
© Copyright 2004 Novello & Compandy Limited.
All Rights Reserved. International Copyright Secured.
Reproduced by permission.

As unexpectedly as the march arrives, it is over – perhaps even comparably to Mahler's original march connotation in his symphonies. Delicately, Arnold establishes a pianissimo cluster texture in con sordino strings from $\boxed{O}$, based on the harmonic B-minor scale. In the full score the schematic canonic structure creates the notion of apparently being uncomplicated; however, the tonal impact is remarkably well chosen in this dramatic context. Because of the withholding of tension as a result of the sudden pianissimo, Arnold could then return to the subject. In conclusion, he could recapitulate the earlier intimacy by using a thinner orchestration, thereby escaping the danger of wearing out the march.[54]

Now, at $\boxed{P}$, the initial development can be described as coda-like, while at $\boxed{R}$ the orchestration becomes even thinner and the subject entry in the horn is supported by the same accompanying thirds from the beginning of the movement, now scored for the violins in quavers. Shortly before the end, Arnold quotes the march again, but this quotation probably has much more to do with a possible reference line on which Arnold wants to focus; because of the pp-dynamics, one cannot compare this passage to the layout in $\boxed{K}$. The movement closes on a high B-minor triad in the violins and the viola.

---

[54] "Ironically" said: there is always this danger in the case of a march, whether it is by Arnold or not...

Figure 18 *Symphony No. 2, opus 40*, **third movement, letter** O

Mitchell refers, in his discussion of the 2nd Symphony, to three of Mahler's concrete symphonic works: his 1st, 4th, and 5th Symphonies. He states that Arnold uses Mahler's symbolism but achieves a completely different and new meaning. The extent to which this judgement is correct, under what circumstances Arnold falls back on Mahler's topoi and conventions, and what is purely "Arnoldish" shall now be scrutinised.

If one compares the symbolism of Arnold's 2nd Symphony with the specifically mentioned Mahler symphonies, the resemblance is really remarkable. And, even if Mitchell did only mean his statement concerning Arnold's ability "to turn them inside out" as a metaphor, the differences between the two composers must be considered.

On the one hand, Mahler's symbolism-afflicted topoi – the loudly yelling C-clarinets, the rough horn-calls from the distance – are a significant sign of Mahler's real love of nature, his Bohemian roots. In spite of these popular aspects, he still always aims at creating real, artistic music and ties that in with an advanced compositional technique. Mahler conceives contrapuntal and syntactical structures so entwined with each other that they emancipate themselves from their pure folk music origins. We **don't** want to state that Arnold was not able to write proper counterpoint: Arnold's reception of „populärmusikalischen Tendenzen" (MOSELER 2002:202) *("popular music tendencies")* can be regarded as open and direct. His tunes, as for example the second subject of his *Concerto for Guitar and Orchestra, opus 67* (1957) or even the fugato theme of the last movement of his 2nd Symphony, are transferred into a context in which they are clearly visible and in which they are not encoded.

On the other hand, in contrast to Mahler's decisive statements, a certain programme is absent from Arnold's symphonies: „...In den Symphonien entwickelt Arnold einen höchst suggestiven Personalstil, der folgerichtig einer weiteren Programmatik nicht bedarf: keine einzige Symphonie trägt einen Titel..." (MOSELER 2002:202). *("...In his symphonies, Arnold develops an extremely suggestive personal style which consistently does not need a programme: no symphony has a title...").* Although Arnold admits that in the case of programmatic works like concert overtures he would at first focus on an emotional idea rather on a musical one – the thematic ideas would then come by themselves[55] – his symphonies are predominated in terms of absolute music. Mahler writes absolute music as well; however, in contrast to Arnold, Mahler's programmatic restraint is proved by his own programme notes and countless letters, suggesting a pictorial and programmatic world.[56]

Is Arnold maybe trying to tell us – in spite of his use of absolute compositional form principles – a story?

---

[55] See Arnold's answer in the conversation with Murray Schafer in 1963 and the author's conclusion in the following chapters.

[56] *cf.* Floros's statements on the genesis of Mahler's programme in his 1st Symphony (FLOROS 1985:25 et seqq.).

Angerer's statements on the irony of the convention and the humorous totality in Mahler's 4th Symphony shall now be our focus. Angerer distinguishes three types of narrative starts: den „episch-distanzierenden", den „dramatisch-beteiligenden" (ANGERER 1994:562-565) und „...die beiden anderen als wohlvertraute Konventionen voraus[setzt] und... mit ihnen sein ironisches Spiel [treibt]" (ANGERER 1994:566) *(the "epic-outdistancing", "dramatic-involving" and a third one which [expects] "...both others as conventions [play]...with them its ironic game".*

He takes up the third narrative type, which he found in Luigi Malerbas's novels, and transfers this to Mahler's 4th Symphony. He questions Mahler in almost a heretical way: „...MAHLERs Vierte...besteht - mehr als noch als jede seiner anderen Schöpfungen - nur aus Konventionen, aus der künstlichen Zusammenfügung traditioneller Klischees oder - etwas wertfreier ausgedrückt - aus altbekannten musikalischen Topoi...Der Komponist zitiert nicht Themen, sondern Tonfälle, traditionelle Wendungen, Satztypen und Formschemata. MAHLER komponiert um die letzte Jahrhundertwende ein Stück, *als ob* er noch das Idiom der Wiener Klassischen Symphonie des ausgehenden 18. Jahrhunderts spräche...Warum komponiert denn jemand eine Symphonie aus klassizistischen Topoi, wenn es ihm offenbar weder um eine neue Klassizität noch um die Verherrlichung alter Zeiten geht? MAHLER zitiert Konventionen, um das von jenen Konventionen ursprünglich Transportierte nachdrücklich zu desavouieren, die Topoi selbst ihrer Scheinhaftigkeit zu überführen und seiner im Grunde mystischen romantischen Ironie dienstbar zu machen."

He continues: „...Der erste Satz ist...wohl MAHLERs schulgerechtester Sonatensatz, der...in praktisch allen Punkten der allbekannten Lehrbuchform entspricht, und zwar genauer, als dies bei irgendeinem anderen bedeutenden Werk der österreichisch-deutschen Musik in dieser Zeit zu beobachten wäre. Schon die Willfähigkeit, mit der sich MAHLER...hier den Konventionen der akademischen Schule unterwirft, macht freilich stutzig..." (ANGERER 1994:567-568) *("...Mahler's fourth...consists – more than his other creations – only of conventions, of the artificial addition of traditional stereotypes or – expressed a little more freely – of well-known musical topoi...The composer does not quote themes, but* Tonfälle, *traditional idioms, voicing structures and form patterns. MAHLER composes a piece around the turn of the century, as if he still spoke the idiom of the Viennese classical symphony of the outgoing 18th century...Why, then, does somebody compose a symphony based on classicistic topoi if he apparently does not strive for a new sort of classicism nor for the glory of former times? MAHLER quotes conventions to disavow the originally emphatically disseminated idea about those conventions; to find the topoi guilty of even their appearance, making them basically servile to his mystic romantic irony...The first movement is...probably Mahler's most academic and most correct movement in sonata form, corresponding...in practically all points to the well-known textbook form, namely more exactly than would be observed with any other significant work of Austrian-German music from this time. Already*

Mahler's will…in which he obeys the conventions of the academic school, may, admittedly, arouse one's suspicion…"

The author's point of view is that Arnold proceeds in a certain way with classical form patterns related to Mahler, as Angerer has indicated. Although this issue will be even more decisively examined within the scope of this research, the following can already be stated in the case of Arnold's 2nd Symphony. First, Arnold uses conventions comparable to Mahler (sonata form, periodicity of subjects) and the specific Mahlerian topoi (e.g., humorous reminiscences, folk music influences, insistence on tunes).

This is stated without prejudice with regard to Mahler – the intention is not to disqualify Mahler's unique compositional position. But Arnold's perception of conventions in general differs from Mahler's. Arnold was either not as well trained in these conventions as Mahler was, or, Arnold does not pay attention to the authenticity of well-known musical topoi. He is not interested in them, so he creates authentic, new, unique, and personal symphonic works.

Second, Arnold generally prefers the much freer form of fantasy and often makes use of it even in his sonata-modelled works. The impact of this – the creation of an episodic effect rather than a strictly developed work of the old school – is viewed by Arnold as a risk. But we must limit this interpretation; it cannot be applied to any of Arnold's symphonic works although the previously discussed third movement of the 2nd Symphony impressively demonstrates his compositional stringency.

The fact that Arnold's symphonic works, despite their absolute formal principles, create narrative connotations for their listeners should not be overlooked. This narrative element is used to create an emotional background, almost like film music's underscoring technique. Arnold understands how to create music of overwhelming joy (a large part of the final textures of the concert overtures show this), irony, humour (*A Grand, Grand Festival Overture*), and, in particular, melancholy and depression as outlined especially in the slow movements of his 9th Symphony. Musical symbols are quoted in a striking or functional way, e.g., the cuckoo and the nightingale in the *Toy Symphony, opus 62*. However, in comparison to Mahler, this symbolism is not the essence of the work, and programmatic texts, often chosen by Mahler as a frame for his symphonies, are hardly ever found in the concertante of Arnold's oeuvre.

What do Mahler and Arnold have in common in terms of their personalities? Except for superficial common characteristics – being composers and conductors/instrumentalists (Arnold as a trumpet player and a conductor of his own works and Mahler as probably the more experienced conductor) – the deeply critical perception of their works and the critics' stress on their popular-music tendencies unite them, cloaking both in the implication of banality. If this stereotyped thinking has been overcome in Mahler's case by the musicological research into his works and by Adorno's writings, it is extremely interesting to quote (keeping in mind Mitchell's support of Arnold) Schönberg's statements about Mahler. The reader may become involved in a mind game of substituting the name Mahler with that of Arnold:

"...Here I must confess that I, too, at first considered Mahler's themes banal...I had found Mahler's themes banal, although the whole work had always made a profound impression on me...if they were really banal I should find them far more banal today than formerly. For banal means rustic, and describes something which belongs to a low grade of culture...Incredibly irresponsible is another accusation made against Mahler: that his themes are unoriginal. In the first place, art does not depend upon the single component part alone; therefore music does not depend upon the theme. For the work of art, like every living thing, is conceived as a whole...The inspiration is not the theme but the whole work. And it is not the one who writes a good theme who is inventive, but the one to whom a whole symphony occurs at once. But in the second place, these themes are original. Naturally, he who looks at only the first four notes will find reminiscences. But he behaves as foolishly as one who looks for original words in an original poem...the small form which we call a theme ought never to be the only yardstick for the large form...And this must also be possible in music; with the most ordinary successions of tones one ought to be able to say the most extraordinary things. Mahler does not need that as an excuse...Mahler's themes are original in the highest sense, when one observes with what fantasy and art, with what wealth of variation there comes out of a few such tones an endless melody..." (SCHÖNBERG 1984:455-458).

Even if some of Arnold's subjects do not, at first glance, seem original, Arnold's compositional technique is, as a general rule, usually marked by high compositional quality. Whether one likes this style or not, it is nevertheless an aesthetic enigma and deserves a personal response from all.

3.3 Sibelius

Arnold described his compositional aesthetic in two important statements in the article, "I Think of Music In Terms of Sounds", and in his conversation with Murray Schafer. He also stressed the importance of Sibelius in his work. If in the article he generally refers to form structures ("...one can find in some late Sibelius works perfect unity and form in performance, and yet to the eye there is no apparent connection at all between the musical statements..." [ARNOLD 1956:168]), in his talk with Schafer, he reveals his compositional techniques, which he derived from Sibelius:

"...The greatest single influence in my music has been Sibelius. It's no doubt unfashionable to admit that. Still, I think the finest piece of music written in the last fifty years is Sibelius's fourth symphony, and it never ceases

79

to amaze me from the formal point of view…Sibelius's ideas of form have impressed me deeply. I can quote an example. In the development sections of his symphonies, Sibelius makes a habit of letting the strings run up and down in scale-like passages or tremolos while little bits of the principal themes are thrown about among the woodwinds or brass. The development section of my overture *Beckus the Dandipratt* is constructed in a similar way, but over a side-drum roll. The roll has taken the place of the tremolos, but the principle is the same…" (SCHAFER 1963:151).

The analysis of the Beckus subject from *Beckus the Dandipratt, opus 5*, reveals another influence on Arnold's ability to show roguish humour. The choice of the cornet as a solo instrument could be interpreted as a French influence or orientation towards the English brass band – and, at the same time, "Papa Strauss" beats jocularly on Arnold's shoulders, asking, "where has Till remained?"

Figure 19 *Beckus the Dandipratt* cornet subject

Reproduced by permission Alfred Lengnick & Co Ltd.

The relevant place in *Beckus the Dandiprattt, opus 5*, can be found relatively easily. Seven bars before O, a roll on the side drum appears, announced by a preceding short solo-intermezzo between the kettledrum and the side drum, which diminishes bit by bit in the following bars into a pianissimo. One bar after O, Arnold begins to pick single parts of the subjects and present them consecutively in the following manner: directly at O in the bassoons (paraphrased without the up-beat); then the trumpets/cornet, which are supported by pizzicati violins and the fortissimo bass note B natural in the low woodwinds, the low brass instruments, the contrabasses, and the violoncelli; then single fragments afterwards in the woodwinds (flutes and oboes in unison).

From P on, he substitutes the side-drum roll with a regular tremolo in the strings (without contrabasses), tremolling a B-minor triad in first inversion. This is answered by fragmentary throw-ins of the subject in single woodwind instruments (the first flute low-scored, then an extremely high first bassoon). Arnold continues this use of fragmentary pieces in contrast to the homogeneous scored exposition. Six bars after S, the entire

80

subject is stated in E-flat major for the first time in the low string section (violas, cellos, and contrabasses); the violins later jump in as well.[57]

If we now look at Sibelius's 4th Symphony, however, it becomes evident that a **literal** transfer, as Arnold has suggested in his remark, is not possible, and Sibelius's influence on Arnold does inspire continuing questions.

The particular British fascination with Sibelius, which can be seen as a kind of determinant in the perception history, is expressed for the first time in Cecil Gray's full-scale study, *A Survey of Contemporary Composition* (1924), which evoked (in Tavaststjerna's opinion) a similarly contrary way of thinking, as in the case of Adorno and his opposing composers, Stravinsky and Schönberg: „...Gray hatte...damit in England großes Aufsehen erregt, vielleicht nicht so sehr, weil er darin Modegrößen wie Strawinsky und Skrjabin in leicht herabwürdigendem Ton behandelte, sondern eher, weil er u.a. Sibelius und Bartók in den Himmel lobte...." (TAVASTJERNA 2005:296). *"...Gray had created...a sensation in England, maybe not because he treated the fashionable composers Stravinsky and Skrjabin in a slightly derogatory manner, but rather because he praised Sibelius and Bartók and others so highly...".*

However, Adorno is still much stronger in his aesthetic judgement of Sibelius than his critical remarks on Stravinsky could possibly reveal. In his gloss 'Glosse über Sibelius', published in 1938, he takes up this English enthusiasm and questions at first the full score and his auditive impression without prejudice – at least, he states: „...Man wird neugierig und hört sich einige der Hauptwerke, etwa die vierte und fünfte Symphonie an. Zuvor studiert man die Partituren. Sie sehen dürftig und böotisch aus, und man meint, das Geheimnis könne sich nur dem leibhaftigen Hören erschließen. Aber der Klang ändert nichts am Bild. Das sieht so aus: es werden, als ‚Themen', irgendwelche völlig unplastischen und trivialen Tonfolgen aufgestellt, meistens nicht einmal ausharmonisiert, sondern unisono mit Orgelpunkten, liegenden Harmonien und was sonst nur die fünf Notenlinien hergeben, um logischen akkordischen Fortgang zu vermeiden. Diesen Tonfolgen widerfährt sehr früh ein Unglück, etwa wie einem Säugling, der vom Tisch herunterfällt und sich das Rückgrat verletzt. Sie können nicht richtig gehen. Sie bleiben stecken. An einem unvorhergesehenen Punkt bricht die rhythmische Bewegung ab: der Fortgang wird unverständlich. Dann kehren die simplen Tonfolgen wieder, verschoben und verbogen, ohne doch von der Stelle zu kommen. Diese Teile gelten den Apologeten für beethovenisch: aus dem Unbedeutenden, Nichtigen eine Welt schaffen. Aber sie ist derer würdig, in der wir leben: roh zugleich und

---

[57] To speak of a recapitulation within the scope of the sonata form, however, would lead to a misinterpretation. Arnold loves to use subject entries crosswise, either literally or marginally modified, so that in the author's opinion they belong to the development. At Ⅴ (subject entry of the first flute), one could speak of the beginning recapitulation – but the general pause 16 bars after Ⅴ does question this impression, too. However, the following 12 bars clearly lead to the final clauses so that the impression that Arnold uses a modified sonata form (exposition-development section-recapitulation-coda) is manifested in his concert overture.

mysteriös, abgegriffen und widerspruchsvoll, altbekannt und undurchsichtig. Wieder sagen die Apologeten, das eben bezeuge die Inkommensurabilität des formschaffenden Meisters, der keine Schablonen gelten lasse. Aber man dem die inkommensurablen Formen nicht, der offensichtlich keinen vierstimmigen Satz auszumessen vermag....Es ist die Originalität der Hilfslosigkeit: vom Schlag jener Amateure, die fürchten, Kompositionsstunden zu nehmen, um nicht ihr Eigentümliches zu verlieren...Über Sibelius als Komponisten wären so wenig Worte zu verlieren wie über solche Amateure...Man kann sich gut vorstellen, dass er nach seinen deutschen Kompositionsstudien dorthin mit berechtigten Inferioritätsgefühlen zurückkam, wohl bewusst der Tatsache, dass ihm weder einen Choral auszusetzen, noch einen ordentlichen Kontrapunkt zu schreiben vergönnt war....Wahrscheinlich war keiner erstaunter als er zu entdecken, dass sein Versagen als Gelingen, sein Nicht-Können als Müssen gedeutet wurde. Schließlich hat er es wohl selbst geglaubt und brütet nun [1938] jahrelang über der achten Symphonie, als ob es die Neunte wäre...." (ADORNO 2003:1411 7ff [cf. GS 17, p. 247ff]).

"...You may be curious and listen to some of his major works, for example the Fourth and Fifth symphonies. You study the score beforehand. It seems sparse and dull, and you think that listening to it will unlock its secrets. But it sounds no different than it looks. You hear a series of unimaginative, meaningless tunes that are supposed to represent the 'themes'. Most of the time these are not even accompanied, just played in unison with pedal points and overlying harmonies and whatever else you can get on the stave to avoid any kind of logical chord progression. Misfortune soon befalls these melodies. Like a baby who has rolled off his changing table and hurt his back – he can't move, so he stays put. Unexpectedly the rhythmical movement comes to a halt. The continuation becomes inaudible. Then the simplistic tunes return, this time shifted and bent around, but still not actually going anywhere. Apologists regard such sections as Beethovenian because a world is created from the insignificant, from nothingness. Indeed they are full of praise for this world in which we simultaneously experience the raw and the mysterious, the fatigued and the contradictory, the knowable and the obtuse. The apologists go on saying that this just goes to show how incommensurable he is, this unparalleled master of form. And yet one who is obviously incapable of gauging a four-note phrase...It smacks of cluelessness, just like those amateurs who worry that taking composition classes will mean losing their individuality...There is as little to say about Sibelius' compositions as about such amateurs...One can well imagine that he left his composition lessons in Germany with feelings of justifiable inferiority, knowing full well that setting a chorale or writing an ordered counterpoint were beyond him...He was probably more surprised than anyone to discover that his failure was celebrated as success, his inability seen as intention. In the end he actually believed this himself and has now [1938] spent years brooding over his Eighth Symphony as if it were his Ninth...".

Even if we ignore Adorno's obvious polemic – Finnscher chooses to describe it with the expression „überaus töricht" (*"quite foolish"*) in his Sibelius article in the MGG (music encyclopedia) – not much of substance remains. Adorno dislikes the fragmentary nature of Sibelius's subjects, which seemingly follow the path of conventions and traditions of symphonic development in the classical and romantic periods. If tonality in general may be used as a compositional means – almost as a *historical* means compared to the contemporary development of the second Viennese school – then, nevertheless, please follow the rules and score the music in a well-arranged four-part writing....[58]

Adorno does not even shy away from still stronger criticism, and vehemently questions Sibelius's symphonic aesthetic: „...Der Erfolg von Sibelius ist ein Störungssymptom des musikalischen Bewusstseins. Das Erdbeben, das in den Dissonanzen der großen neuen Musik seinen Ausdruck fand, hat die altmodische kleine nicht verschont. Sie ist rissig und schief geworden. Aber während man vor den Dissonanzen flüchtet, hat man bei den falschen Dreiklängen Zuflucht gesuchet. Die falschen Dreiklänge: Strawinsky hat sie auskomponiert. Er hat durch hinzugesetzte falsche Noten demonstriert, wie falsch die richtigen geworden. Bei Sibelius klingen schon die reinen falsch. Er ist ein Strawinsky wider Willen. Nur hat er weniger Talent...Symphonien sind keine tausend Seen; auch wenn sie tausend Löcher haben..." (ADORNO 2003:14120ff [cf. GS 17, p. 250ff]).

"...The success of Sibelius is symptomatic of a breakdown in musical understanding. The old school has been unable to escape from the quaking dissonances in major works of new music. The music is cracked and flawed. But those fleeing the dissonance have sought shelter in false triads, as favoured by Stravinsky. By adding false notes, he was able to show how false the right ones were. In Sibelius, even the proper notes sound wrong. He is a reluctant Stravinsky. Only he has less talent...Finland may be the land of a thousand lakes, but no symphony should have a thousand holes."

Let's now leave Adorno's boxing ring, although this short excursion is important to demonstrate one prominent point: the deviationaism of conventional topoi and the canonical grounds of the symphonic form have not become a point of criticism in Arnold's case alone. However, the annotators' views seem to change the moment they become aware of the lack of correspondence with tradition, and, as a consequence, they apparently start to focus on this singular (and sometimes minor) point.

Indeed, Sibelius's 4th Symphony is unusual in its syntax and form as well as in its concept of motifs and subjects. It is not just the tritone

---

[58] What would Adorno have said if he had reviewed Arnold as a composer?

relation between "icy A minor to glowing Eb major" (WHITTALL 2004:54) that matters here; the tritone itself is the constituting element of the first subject, used here even without its implied tonic note A that can be deduced only in retrospect. Indeed, the general characteristic style of the harmonic language is still marked by triads; however, harmonic progressions are not used in the customary sense of a classical key plan. Instead, they are oriented modally and have a colouring effect, too. Antokoletz's interpretation shall be reviewed in this connection: "...While triads move within the static framework of the diatonic folk modes, which together with ostinato-like thematic patterns and sustained chords contribute significantly to the national flavor of the work, theses modes often acquire an exotic coloring through their local transformations into octatonic and whole-tone formations..." (ANTOKOLETZ 2001:298f).

Antokoletz has provided a clear and formal overview of Sibelius's 4th Symphony (ANTOKOLETZ 2001:299-300). What he works through extremely well is Sibelius's preference for singular thematic ideas, in contrast to the pure elaboration of two subjects that act symbiotically with other (as in the classicist epoch). He describes a total of five different main thematic ideas (a-f); while a and b portray an antecedent-consequent structure of the first subject (b. 1-31), and the second subject is represented by the letters d, e, and f (b. 31-40), c is transitional material that leads to the second subject (b. 29f). If one views the development section of the 4th Symphony analytically, what Arnold meant by referring to "Sibelius's habit" becomes evident for the first time. Sibelius's development section is marked by a juxtaposition of the different thematic motifs not in the consecutive original juxtaposition, but flexible in terms of juxtaposition: thus, in the beginning of the development section (b. 55 et seqq.), the consequent of the first subject appears in the low strings (b, cf. b. 6 solo violoncello), followed by a subject fragment taken from the second subject (d, b. 66 et seqq.). This is followed directly by the antecedent of the first subject (a, b. 72 et seqq.). Arnold's description of Sibelius's approach ("letting the strings run up and down in scale-like passages or tremolos") must be qualified – his own adaptation of this procedure, letting the subject fragments appear above a side-drum roll, is not at all as advanced as Sibelius's.

Arnold regards Sibelius's 4th Symphony as an important monument in contemporary music. While Dahlhaus has already recognised the progressiveness of this 4th Symphony in his ponderings on Sibelius, Tim Howell provides a new, particularly positive view in his study, "Sibelius the Progressive".[59] Howell notes that the core of Sibelius's composition technique in his 4th Symphony is repetition. He classifies this core point into two characteristics, "the use of repetition patterns" in general (HOWELL 2001:42) and "the use of large-scale transposed repetition" in particular (HOWELL 2001:44). In the latter he is referring to the literal repetition and the transposition of an idea onto another scale degree. Howell's description seems amazingly well suited to one of

---

[59] Thanks to Schönberg...

Arnold's symphonic works: "...Repetition patterns in Sibelius range from ostinati (associated with linear time); they encompass the literal, the varied, and the sequential presentation of particular cells, with elements of immediate or delayed, metrically regular or irregular, repetition thrown in for good measure in a range of permutations..." His conclusions shall not be dismissed in this connection, either, however; the interplay, the weight, and the "staticness" expressed by the repetition pattern can apply equally to Sibelius **and** to Arnold, even if Howell did not initially intended this comparison to be applied to Arnold: "...Musical continuity (or, indeed, discontinuity) emerges from such patterning and a balance between essentially what is static and what is dynamic (and a play on the illusion and reality of both of these) is carefully exploited..." (HOWELL 2001:43).

Furthermore, another of Howell's thoughts shall now be discussed in terms of Arnold: "The concept of Sibelius using the same material placed in differing temporal contexts as part of an underlying variation process..." (HOWELL 2001:45). The possibility of completely turning around the meaning of the thematic material through proportional processing techniques (augmentation, diminution) as well as by drastic tempo changes is assimilated in Arnold's 9th Symphony from two points of view. On the one hand, it is the dramatic, literal repetition of the beginning of the first movement at the end of the recapitulation, now in larger note values, as well as in a dramatically slowed tempo. The latter changes the effect of the piece completely.[60] Arnold also has a tendency to compose more works with a lento character. This allows Arnold to focus on a single tone and its character. He is also able to describe emotional pain musically by using simply an intense, slower tempo.[61]

As already mentioned, Arnold was fascinated by Sibelius's 4th Symphony; however, he did not intend to create a copy or imitation (pastiche) of Sibelius. Arnold understands Sibelius as a style model and is aware of the composition techniques that Sibelius uses to create an ambivalent effect in the listener. Instead, Arnold wants to compose a comprably impressive symphonic opus. Almost in the manner of a composition pupil, he extracts the compositional elements (tritone relation, subject-fragmentation technique, repetition as a universal compositional style method), adapts them, and in doing so apparent becomes an effigy of Sibelius – but only marginally.

The use of the tritone relation, which Sibelius uses as a system-immanent compositional means in the first subject (C-F sharp), is not incorporated literally into the subject of Arnold's 2nd Symphony. But it can be found in the constellation of the key of the first movement (here, E flat-A major) of the 2nd Symphony. Nevertheless, in contrast to Sibelius, Arnold begins with the pastoral, "glowing" E-flat-major tonality in order to modulate later to A major, the key of the second subject. It creates almost

---

[60] See also the author's statements in the chapter on the 9th Symphony.

[61] The intepretation of the 9th Symphony by Andrew Penny can be mentioned in this connection: even Penny does not dare to execute Arnold's original tempos slightly faster than marked in the score.

the notion – only hypothetically formulated – that Arnold had put the task to himself to compose a new symphony marked by Sibelius and Mahler, with all its implications and challenges, with all its quasi-schematism combined with the greatest possible freedom to do anything he wished in regard to his musical subjects. To call him the English Sibelius is to label him the English Shostakovitch or to view him as the absolute Mahler – but this does not actually matter. Arnold is like a painter and thus relates to his artist's tools, the paintbrush and the colour palette. Having probably studied the techniques of his own masters countless times – even experiencing them physically as a trumpet player in the orchestra – he owned, in spite of his young age, a full and distinctive compositional colour palette and chose the masters as a starting point only to finally emancipate himself from them in such an exceptional work as his 2nd Symphony.

3. Understanding the Concept of "Tradition" and Early Symphonic Writing: From Mahlerian Scenery to Arnold's Independence from Sibelius

3. Understanding the Concept of "Tradition" and Early Symphonic Writing: From Mahlerian Scenery to Arnold's Independence from Sibelius

4. British Contemporary Music: Classical Thinking, Progress, Musical Life, the Market Economy, the General Public, and Aesthetic Categorisation within the British Modern Age: The Construction of Arnold's Image

„...Der Fortschritt hat seine Handlanger. Fortschrittsüchtige,
Fortschrittgläubige, Fortschrittmächtige, Fortschritttüchtige -
Fortschrittdogmatiker, Fortschrittgewinnler, sogar Fortschrittkritiker..."
Nikolaus A. Huber *(HUBER 1998:37)*

"...Progress has its odd-job men. People addicted to progress, believers in progress, powerful figures in progress, progress competents, progress dogmatists, people benefiting from progress, even critics of progress..." *Nikolaus A. Huber.*

„...Jeder ästhetische Diskurs ist immer auch einer in historischen
Dimensionen, eingedenk, dass auch ein Diskurs über die Geschichte der
Ästhetik selber historisch ist..." *Renate Reschke (RESCHKE 2004:13)*

"Every aesthetic discourse is also a discourse in historical dimensions, recalling that a discourse about the history of the aesthetics is also historical in itself..." Renate Reschke.

"...Nor does 'absolutely true' mean true independently of any context. We can only judge the world from within some kind of framework...Elephants may be sacred for you but not for me, if this represents a difference between our ways of signifying them. But it cannot be true that elephants are sacred in the same way that they really have four legs...Cultures make sense of the world in different ways, and what some see as a fact others do not; but if truth simply means truth-for-us, then there can be no conflict between us and other cultures, since truth is equally just truth-for-them..." Terry Eagleton *(EAGLETON 2003:107)*

"...Der Komponist, der erfährt, wie seine Musik in erster Linie nach der
Novität seiner Mittel - die ihm doch nur Zweck sind - ihre Beurteilung erhält,
sehnt sich nach dem Rezipienten, den er mit seiner Musik 'berühren' kann,
dem Rezipienten, der nicht nur in der Lage ist 'gerührt' zu sein, dem
Rezipienten in einer veränderten Gesellschaft mithin, deren Kunstverständnis
weit über dem von Kunst als Luxus angesiedelt ist, einer Gesellschaft, die
Konzeption der Utopie 'Kunst' als Teil der eigenen Utopie begreifen kann..."
Manfred Trojahn *(TROJAHN 1981:86)*

4. British Contemporary Music: Classical Thinking, Progress, Musical Life, the Market
Economy, the General Public, and Aesthetic Categorisation within the British Modern Age:
The Construction of Arnold's Image

*"... A composer experiencing that his music is primarily perceived on the
novelty of its means – which are, nevertheless, only a purpose for him –
longs for the recipient whom he can 'touch' with his music, for the
recipient who is not only able to be 'stirred', for the recipient in a
consequently changed society, whose art appreciation is much more
settled in terms of art as a luxury, a society understanding the concept of
the utopian 'art' as a part of its own utopia..." Manfred Trojahn*

The twentieth century and its serious music, in the opinion of the
English musicologist Arnold Whittall, it is the age of "co-existence,
opposition or interaction of tonal (traditional) and post-tonal (progressive)
composition..." (WHITTALL 1997:144). Until the nineteenth century the
image of style as common sense was prevalent among composers of the
same epoch,[62] in the twentieth century we are confronted with rapid
stylistic development. This is based on two characteristic features:
invariability and progress. During preceding centuries there were only a
marginal number of individuals who "offended" stylistic conventions –
consider Frescobaldi's (1583-1643) chromaticism or Anton Reicha's
(1770-1832) odd contrapuntal fugues showing a systematic concept of
fugue writing, the subject based upon a single note or a triad[63] –
contemporary twentieth-century composers seem to distinguish themselves
with their unique personal style. At least, every member of this special
curia seemed to enjoy that image very much.

Furthermore, progress is always influenced by cultural space and
sociological value systems. In particular, progress often reflects
considerations of limited geographical space.[64] Leading a discussion about
several works composed in the same year or even in the same month
without bearing in mind their special context (regional and cultural
background) is an almost impossible task. Moreover, such a procedure
would misjudge the importance of the cultural identity of the specific piece
of music. Even if this question were answered, the diversity as well as the
simultaneousness of styles in the twentieth century creates the notion of
the sword of Damocles on musicological and music-theoretical analysis.
One would be caught in the dilemma of being able to refer only to a single

---

[62] The concept of "style" as "stylus" has been used in former times, often synonymous with
composition in general, for example, in Christoph Bernhard's *Tractatus compositionis
augmentatis* (1657).

[63] In his contemporaries' eyes, they may have evoked the image of madness!

[64] Guido Heldt discusses in his article "The first symphonies – Britten, Walton and Tippett the
same problem: „...Wenn Gattungsgeschichte im Verdacht steht, zum Affirmativen,
Kanonischen und Exklusionistischen zu neigen..., könnten man beim Versuch, sie dennoch zu
beschreiben, gerade bei den Schwierigkeiten ansetzen, bei den Widerständen, die
unordentliche Wirklichkeit den historiographischen Kategorisierungsversuchen entgegensetzt,
und bei der Abhängigkeit der resultierenden Geschichtsbilder von Erkenntnisinteressen und
Frageperspektiven..." (HELDT 2003:84). *("...If the history of categorisation is suspected to have a canonical
and exclusive trend toward the affirmative, one could begin describing the difficulties, the opposition of disordered
reality in contrast to historical categorisation attempts, and the dependence of the resultant historical image on
knowledge interests interrogative perspectives...")*

4. British Contemporary Music: Classical Thinking, Progress, Musical Life, the Market
Economy, the General Public, and Aesthetic Categorisation within the British Modern Age:
The Construction of Arnold's Image

work separately, or being unable to categorise at all. Or, is this not the
case?

The insulated nature of Great Britain could have led to the fact
that British music developed far from the influence of continental Europe.
The argument of geographic separation may be discussed in the context of
a single phenomenon, but when given more precise consideration this
argument is superficial and unsuitable. The argument that the majority of
continental Europe's modern music was unknown in Great Britain around
1900 can only be termed an incredible tale. Numerous composers like
Hubert Parry and Charles Stanford[65] spent a large part of their education in
Germany. Despite the fact that one cannot speak of real, progressive
contemporary British music at the beginning of the twentieth century in
terms of the Second Viennese School, the Britons were well aware of their
continental contemporaries. Looking at the symphonic works of Arnold
Bax, Gordon Jacob, Arnold Bliss, or Bernhard van Dieren underlines
Schaarwächter's notion that composers responded to the
„Herausforderungen der Tonalitätserweiterung" (SCHAARWÄCHTER
1994:335) ("challenges of the expansion of tonality").
Therefore, possible motives for the still noticeably more
conservative compositional style of British composers in the twentieth
century must be deduced from other factors.

The question of special musical style elements of a nation or, more exactly,
of the "Englishness" of British music is somewhat comic in nature. No treatise about
British music misses the famous/infamous statement by Oscar A. H. Schmitz from
1914. He summarises it with a very general and much too simplified, formula: „...das
einzige Kulturvolk ohne eigene Musik (Gassenhauer[66] ausgenommen)..."[67] (SCHMITZ
1914:28). ("... the only cultural people without their own music (except for popular tunes)...").
Schaarwächter prominently discusses this quotation and describes it as
follows: „...Legende, die sich – zumindest in Deutschland, aber auch bei zahlreichen
Briten – bis auf den heutigen Tag weitgehend erhalten hat..." (SCHAARWÄCHTER
1994:31). ("a legend remaining – at least in Germany, but also in the opinion of numerous
Britons –to a great extent up to the present...").

---

[65] cf. Walton's statement: "...Die bedeutendsten britischen Komponisten dieser Zeit, Hubert
Parry (1848-1918) und Charles Stanford (1852-1924), hatten beide in Deutschland
studiert...und waren später gleichzeitig Dozenten am Royal College sowie Ordinarii in Oxford
bzw. Cambridge. Der Einfluss Deutschlands im englischen Musikleben war seit der
Thronbesteigung Queen Victorias erheblich gestiegen...Bis zum Ausbruch des Ersten
Weltkrieges gingen beinahe alle nennenswerten Komponisten englands nach Deutschland,
entweder um zu studieren, oder, wenn das Geld dafür nicht reichte – wie bei Elgar – zumindest
um die Bayreuther Festspiele zu besuchen..." (WALTON 1994:257). ("...The most significant British
composers of this time, Hubert Parry (1848-1918) and Charles Stanford (1852-1924), had both studied in
Germany and were later professors at the same time at the Royal College as well as Ordinarii at Oxford or
Cambridge. The German influence on English musical life had increased considerably since the ascent to the throne
of Queen Victoria...Until the outbreak of World War I, nearly all appreciated English composers went to
Germany, either to study, or, in the case of a lack of money - as in the case of Elgar - at least to visit the Bayreuth
festival...")
[66] „Gassenhauer" is indeed a very strong word in German.
[67] The author notes that he now also feels affiliated to Schaarwächter's juxtaposition...

4. British Contemporary Music: Classical Thinking, Progress, Musical Life, the Market Economy, the General Public, and Aesthetic Categorisation within the British Modern Age: The Construction of Arnold's Image

With regard to a possible definition of what a British composer is, Schaarwächter decisively suggests extending Ernest Walker's definition of English music as "made in England". However, overall, his suggestion is in no way pioneering. Schaarwächter's deduction – see particularly the last paragraph of the following quotation – appears questionable and unscientific:

„...Als britische Komponisten werden bezeichnet:
- Komponisten, die in Großbritannien geboren sind;
- nicht in Großbritannien geborene Komponisten, die in Großbritannien einen wesentlichen Teil ihres Lebens verbrachten; hierbei ist der Grad der 'Britishness' dann jeweils individuell zu bestimmen; sowie
- nicht in Großbritannien geborene Komponisten, die ihre musikalische Entwicklung in Großbritannien erlebten und später aus beruflichen oder anderen Gründen die britischen Inseln verließen; hierunter sind jedoch nicht solche zu verstehen, die ihrem britischem Einfluss kritisch und zweifelnd gegenüberstanden...
Diese Überlegungen folgen zahlreichen Gesprächen mit Briten, die befragt wurden, was sie als britische Komponisten ansehen würden..." (SCHAARWÄCHTER 1994:27-29).

"... As British composers are labelled:

- composers who are born in Great Britain;

- composers who are not born in Great Britain but have spent an essential part of their lives in Great Britain; the degree of the 'Britishness' is hereby determined in each case individually; as well as

- composers who are not born in Great Britain but have experienced a large part of their musical education and development in Great Britain and later left the British Isles because of occupational or other reasons; nevertheless, those who faced the British influence critically shall be excluded...

These considerations follow numerous conversations with Britons who were questioned whom they consider British composers..."

Whereas for instance the Austrian geographic space was marked by a constant change of affiliations to various monarchies,[68] the geographic space of Great Britain can be regarded as quite insulated. Indeed, Malcolm Arnold's fate was predetermined by his birthright, by growing up in the midlands of England and by studying at the Royal College of Music in London, the British music institute par excellence. In certain ways, this probably influenced him in his socialisation as a British composer – Dibelius's idea of the „nationalen Bindung" ("national connection") and the affiliation to certain groups which „[k]eines Nachweises durch formulierte Thesen oder Programme bedürfe..." (DIBELIUS 1998:290) *("do not need to be proved by formulated theses or programmes...")* is appropriate. However, a musical analysis within the humanities, dealing with the stylistic peculiarities of a musical

---

[68] *cf.* the academic statement written with a certain self-mocking undertone by Angerer on the question of the Habsburg multinational state (ANGERER 2006:9).

nation and – as in this case – a particular composer (Arnold), can indeed neglect certain research based on genealogical roots. It is rather important to ask how Arnold behaved in comparison to other British composers. Does he take up, for example, British styles (English dances, Irish dances, Cornish dances, and Welsh dances, which clearly underscore the enormous value he places on his British origins)? Or does he actually oppose these British traditions?

The northern English musicologist Chris Walton, educated at Cambridge and Oxford, offered an explanation to that question in 1994. His proposed explanation shall now be discussed with regard to Malcolm Arnold's particular situation.

In his article „Auf der Suche nach der Moderne in England" *("Searching for the modern age in England")*, Walton devotes himself first to the question of how one can distinguish more modern composers from more conservative composers in twentieth-century England. His argument repeats conventional patterns, but his first postulation pricks one's ear. He does not label the Manchester School of the sixties as the first "school", but states: „...Um die Jahrhundertwende entstand auch die erste 'Schule' in der modernen Musikgeschichte Englands, sie bestand aus fünf Komponisten, die am Konservatorium in Frankfurt studierten: Cyril Scott, Roger Quilter, Norman O'Neill, Balfour Gardiner und der geborene Australier Percy Grainger...". *"...Around the turn of the century the first 'school' originated in the modern history of music in England. It consisted of five composers who had studied at the Frankfurt Conservatory: Cyril Scott, Roger Quilter, Norman O'Neill, Balfour Gardiner and the born-Australian Percy Grainger..."* At the same time Walton underscores that the development of contemporary music around 1900 progressed in exactly the same way as it did in continental Europe, particularly in Germany, Austria, and France: „...Vor dem Ersten Weltkrieg fehlten also keine Voraussetzungen für eine englische Entwicklung der Moderne. Fortschrittliche Komponisten wie Elgar waren keine Außenseiter, sondern ins nationale Musikleben weitgehend integriert. Die zeitgenössische Musik Deutschlands, Frankreichs, Österreichs und Russlands war dank Dirigenten wie Thomas Beecham und Henry Wood gut bekannt..." (WALTON 1994:257-258). *("...Before World War I, no conditions for an English development of contemporary music were absent. Advanced composers like Elgar were not outsiders, but rather integrated to a great extent into the nation's musical life. The contemporary music of Germany, France, Austria and Russia was well known, thanks to conductors like Thomas Beecham and Henry Wood..."*

However, Walton admits that the further development of British music did not run parallel to that of continental Europe. From a German perspective, it could not be regarded as a „...Verlauf in Richtung Fortschritt, Atonaliät und Dodekaphonie..." (WALTON 1994:258) (*"...course in the direction of progress, atonality and dodecaphony..."*).

Walton puts forth the idea of four conditional factors that were responsible for this special, and, from a continental European viewpoint,

4. British Contemporary Music: Classical Thinking, Progress, Musical Life, the Market
Economy, the General Public, and Aesthetic Categorisation within the British Modern Age:
The Construction of Arnold's Image

extremely individual and apparently reactionary development of English
contemporary music. In his first thesis, he points out the early stages of
nationalism in English music, which began about 1900. Walton states that
English musical culture is close to German musical culture, but concludes:
„...dass das Verlangen nach einer eindeutigen einheimischen Musik in
England nicht nur viel später als in anderen europäischen Ländern wuchs,
sondern erst zu jener Zeit entstand, als Englands wirtschaftliche und
militärische Stärke am Abnehmen war. In der Musik vollzog sich dies in
Form der ,Entdeckung' der heimischen Volksmusik" (WALTON 1994:258f).
*("...that the desire for unequivocal local music in England not only
appeared much later than in other European countries, but originated only
when England lost its powerful economic and military strength. In music,
this was reflected as a 'discovery' of domestic folk music..."* Indeed,
Walton's statement is appropriate in relation to the folk music movement
among English composers around 1900. Important composers like Hubert
Parry (1848-1918) or Ralph Vaughan Williams (1872-1958) were
associated with it. Parry even acted as president of the Folk Song Society.
The movement had significant consequences for British composers, who
started to write various tone poems using original English folk tunes or
created similar-sounding tunes of their own. Vaughan Williams's
Greensleeves is probably the most prominent example of this
phenomenon.

Walton's line of thought can be clearly understood up to this
point, but concluding from the broad support for the folk music movement
in Great Britain that it was „...eine[.] Bewegung, die tonale Musik forderte
und die keine Voraussetzung für eine Entwicklung einer englischen
,Moderne' bot..." (WALTON 1994:260). *("...a movement which demanded
tonal music and which offered no conditions for the development of
English 'contemporary music'...")* is too absolute and too simplistic. The
dominance of the national folk music movement may have led to a one-
sided perception among the general public, but writing substantial and
more advanced music was always possible, even at that time. An example
of this is William Walton's *Façade*. The scratchy, irritating, and, for
British ears at that time, apparently indecent musical language, with Edith
Sitwell's nonsensical poems as lyrics, caused a scandal at its first big
public performance in 1923. We do no criticise Chris Walton for his thesis,
but he does not provide a logical explanation for it.

Walton's second thesis brings up a historical side issue that is
initially interesting: World War I „...Von größerer Bedeutung ist jedoch die
Tatsache, dass England im Ersten Weltkrieg eine große Anzahl junger
Männer verlor, die sich in ihrem Einsatz für die zetigenössische Musik gerade
erst profiliert hatten: Der Dirigent Bevin Ellis...der Komponist Ernest
Farrar...der Australier Frederick Kelly...Ein Verlust anderer Art für das
englische Musikleben war Percy Grainger, der wenige Tage nach Ausbruch
des Krieges mit seiner Mutter nach Amerika auswanderte...Hier liegt also der
zweite Grund für die Nichtexistenz einer englischen Moderne: Die
Generation, welch sie hätte gründen können, starb zum großen Teil in der
Schlammwüste von Flandern..." (WALTON 1994:260-261).

("...Nevertheless, it is significant that England lost a large number of young men in World War I who had recently started to distinguish themselves within the circles of contemporary music: the conductor Bevin Ellis...the composer Ernest Farrar...the Australian Frederick Kelly...A loss of another kind for English musical life was Percy Grainger, who had emigrated with his mother to America just a few days after the outbreak of war...This is the second reason for the non-existence of English contemporary music: the generation which could have founded it died in large part in the muddy desert of Flanders...') Walton's argument focuses on the missing generation[69] – and his argument is weighty. There are numerous comparable situations in which wars significantly influenced cultural change. However, in terms of Arnold, this view is not useful. He belonged to the post-World War I generation and was – except for his short military service as a trumpeter and the tragic death of his brother as an airman during World War II – spared the direct personal consequences of the war. One could possibly conclude that a comparable situation caused by World War II could have led to a similar effacement of a generation of composers. However, Walton misjudges the fact that contemporary music from continental Europe had already arrived in Britain, either directly via pupils such as Egon Wellesz or Humphrey Searle or simply through being adopted by younger composers (the Manchester School). These composers, though, operated in niches of public musical life. We cannot deduce from the political and sociological circulation of both world wars why Arnold and other generations (Tippet, born in 1905, and Britten, born in 1913) did not compose in as "advanced" a manner as their "friends" on the continent.

Walton then examines possible institutions in England which often commissioned compositions in the twentieth century. He identifies the Anglican Church as one of the most important institutions; indeed, the composers Benjamin Britten and Michael Tippet had been integrated into the church during their regular education through attending church services and singing in the boys' choir. Both received many commissions from the Anglican Church. Britten's development as a composer is inseparable from his choral work, *A Child is Born*. Other choral music classics like his *A Ceremony of Carols* (1942), *Rejoice in the Lamb* (1943), and *Missa Brevis in D, opus 63* (1959)[70] still play a vital role in the choral life of Great Britain today.

---

[69] The consequences of World War II on the reorganisation of the Federal Republic of Germany can be seen in the average age in the executive administrative service and in legislative positions – Konrad Adenauer was 65 years old when he became Chancellor of Germany.

[70] The monumental *War Requiem* (1961) cannot be left unmentioned here with regards to his use of the classical liturgy. But the performance and the genesis of the work must be seen in the context of Britten's pacifistic background. In addition to the role of *War Requiem* as a national symbol, the solo voices were sung by the German baritone Fischer-Dieskau as well as the English tenor Peter Pears; however, the Russian soprano Galina Wischnewskaja was not allowed to cross the border and the English soprano Heather Harper was substituted for her. Understandably, the Anglican Church had a lesser influence in this respect.

„"...Der dritte Grund ist eine Institution, nämlich die Anglikanische Kirche. Eine große Zahl der bedeutendsten englischen Komponisten der vergangenen hundert Jahre hat in Oxford oder in Cambridge studiert und sich dadurch mit der anglikanischen Musiktradition auseinandersetzen müssen... Diejenigen Komponisten, die an einem Konservatorium studierten, wie z. B. Benjamin Britten oder Michael Tippett, mussten dafür im Internat anglikanische Gottesdienste besuchen und anglikanische Chor- und Orgelwerke wöchentlich, wenn nicht täglich anhören...

Die Musik für die Liturgie der anglikanischen Kirche war und bleibt konservativ...Sie darf nicht atonal klingen, geschweigedenn avantgardistisch, denn der Entscheid, worüber gesungen wird, liegt schlussendlich beim Klerus. Man könnte vermuten, dass ein Komponist, der in seiner Jugend jahrelang anglikanische Musik anhören oder gar singen musste, zu einem gewissen Zeitpunkt gegen sie reagieren werde. Dies ist jedoch in England anscheinend nicht der Fall. Denn kaum ein englischer Komponist, inklusive Atheisten und Agnostiker, hat n i c h t für die Kirche geschrieben...

Kein Komponist wird aus irgendwelchen Gründen dazu gezwungen, für die Kirche zu komponieren, aber jede, der für die Kirche schreiben will, muss seinen eigenen Stil deren Wünschen anpassen...Solche Kompromisse wären für die Vertreter der Moderne in Deutschland kaum akzeptabel gewesen..." (WALTON 1994:261-262).

"...The third reason is an institution, namely the Anglican Church. A large number of the most significant English composers of the past hundred years studied at Oxford or at Cambridge and had to thereby argue about the Anglican musical tradition...Those composers who studied at a conservatory, as, for example, Benjamin Britten or Michael Tippett, had to attend Anglican church services at their boarding schools and to listen to Anglican choral works and organ works weekly, if not daily...

The music for the liturgy of the Anglican Church was, and remains, conservative...It is not allowed to sound atonal, let alone avant-garde, because the decision about what was sung was made by the clergy. One could suppose that a composer who had, for years, listened to or sung Anglican music in his youth might even, at a certain point, rebel against it. Nevertheless, this is apparently not the case in England, since no English composer, including atheists and agnostics, has n o t written for the church...

No composer is forced to compose for the church, but everybody who intends to write for the church must adapt his own style to its wishes...Such compromises would hardly have been satisfactory to the representatives of contemporary music in Germany...".

Although Walton draws some important conclusions, unfortunately his analysis is accompanied, incorrectly, by a basic, simple image. While a composer is of course always influenced by the framework of the institution commissioning a work, the work itself will still be composed to serve its own special purpose. However, to assume that composers developed a so-called "clerical style" for these commissions in order to avoid having to justify themselves to the Anglican Church is an idealistic image.[71] Such an analysis must not overlook the cultural peculiarities of the Anglican Church and Great Britain itself.[72] However, in the case of Arnold's choral works, which consist of at least ten works, it becomes obvious that, contrary to Walton's third thesis, Arnold remains Arnold. He does not amend his style of composition for the church or for other institutions.

The British composer William Walton, who was born in 1902 in Oldham and died in 1983 in Iscia, Italy, is a prime example of the development of the generation of British composers born around 1900. His early musical talent was recognised within the scope of choir school at Christ Church, Oxford. These choir schools continued a medieval tradition based on the principle of apprenticeships; a famous example is Clementi and his apprentices John Field and Johann Baptist Cramer. After graduating from one of the choir schools, which were generally attached to the famous universities in Oxford and Cambridge, a diversified programme of study followed that consisted of music-historic, composition, and practical music courses, and also covered fields such as literature, mathematics, Latin, and/or Greek. After graduation, the scholars received their Bachelor of Arts, and later their Bachelor of Music degrees.

Walton's artistic talent appeared, according to a statement by Thomas Strong, his former dean at Christ Church, not in singing, but in the field of composition (KENNEDY 1989:7). Despite the fact that he passed his music examinations, he failed mathematics and Greek, and later left the university without having graduated. He became acquainted with the Sitwell family, a socially respectable English family that included a great literary talent in the person of Edith Sitwell. The family's readiness to provide him with accommodations and promote him financially gave him access to new social circles and to experiences with contemporary music, in particular with the French music of Les Six and Stravinsky.

Stravinksky, along with Edith Sitwell's poetic studies called *Façade*, inspired Walton to compose the *Façade of Entertainment* for speakers and four instrumentalists in 1921. The premiere took place on 24 January 1922, attended by only a close circle of the Sitwells's friends.

The first big public performance of the work, in 1923, led to a scandal. Walton's musical language, influenced in its pointillism and scanty orchestration by Stravinsky's *L'histoire du Soldat*, forced into a syncope-stressed jazzy "corset" and paradoxically coloured by Sitwell's "nonsense poems", was so diametrically opposed to the putative, traditional English music of Elgar and Vaughan Williams that Walton could be sure of attracting a great deal of attention in the English musical circles.

---

[71] *cf.* Lutoslawki's *Requiem* or Ligeti`s *Lux Aeterna*; even if these compositions were not composed in England, the contour of these works does imply that in fact composers insisted on writing what they wanted to write.
[72] It is a pity that Walton does not consider the immanently important position of the Arts Council or of the BBC after World War II in Great Britain.

The fact that Walton further devoted himself to the form of classical instrumental concerto in 1928/1929 and composed his Concerto for Viola and Orchestra using a far more luxuriant orchestration must not be seen as a step back from Elgar's excess. The harmony had become much more differentiated (see the B-flat major key triad over an 'a'-pedal in the strings), chromatic contrapuntal lines were developed (see the violas in bars 1-9), and Walton's theme of solo viola were typical characteristics of new contemporary music. Aside from movements in seconds, wide interval leaps as minor and major sevenths or ninths (m. 5/6, m. 7/8, m. 11) dominate. His orchestration technique of the early thirties shows that he often assigns contrapuntal textures to the woodwinds, those articulating contrapuntal solistic lines (m. 7 clarinets, m. 8 flutes, rehearsal number 1 oboe, one before rehearsal number 2: bassoon). The string corpus, which at first glance appears to be a very thick structure, is qualified by its dynamics and their articulations (divisi, sul ponticello, contrast between solo and tutti).

Above all, Walton's free, rhapsodic treatment of syntax and form reveals that he has left Elgar's compositional patterns behind him and that he applies techniques taken from European contemporary music. In that sense, he rejects the more conservative forms that his friend Malcolm Arnold used.[73]

In Chris Walton's fourth thesis, he considers a political component for explaining the "non-development" of avant-garde contemporary music. „...Es besteht in England, zumindest seit Vaughan Williams, der Glaube, ein Komponist müsse ein integrales Mitglied der Gesellschaft sein... ("...There is in England, at least since Vaughan Williams, the belief that a composer must be an integral member of society...).

Für Vaughan Williams ist der Künstler kein Führer der Gesellschaft, sondern ihr Diener, eine Haltung, die später auch die Musikästhetik von Benjamin Britten charakterisierte. Schon als Student betrachtete sich Vaughan Williams als Sozialist, seiner enger Freund Gustav Holst wurde mit 21 Jahren Mitglied eines Socialist Club in London...Tippett und Benjamin Britten waren in ihrer Jugend politisch noch aktiver als Holst oder Vaughan Williams, während ein Freund Tippetts, der Komponist Alan Bush, sein Leben lang Kommunist blieb...Rutland Boughton...blieb bis zum russischen Einmarsch in Ungarn Mitglied der kommunistischen Partei..."

("For Vaughan Williams the artist is not a leader of society, but its servant, an outlook which later also characterised the musical aesthetics of Benjamin Britten. As a student, Vaughan Williams already considered himself a Socialist, and his close friend Gustav Holst became a member of a Socialist club in London at the age of 21...Tippett and Benjamin Britten were even more politically active in their youth than Holst or Vaughan Williams, while a friend of Tippett,

---

[73] William Walton, who composed notoriously slowly, received compositional support from Malcolm Arnold in producing the soundtrack for The Battle of Britain (1969). Arnold, who was engaged at first only as a conductor, wrote a large part of the music as a ghostwriter – this can be deduced from viewing the autographs (HARRIS/MEREDITH 2004:278-279).

the composer Alan Bush, remained a life-long Communist...Rutland Boughton...remained a member of the Communist Party up to the Russian invasion of Hungary...")

„Vaughan Williams war, wie im Grunde Holst, Britten und auch Tippett, ein Anhänger jenes viktorianischen, paternalistischen Sozialismus der oberen Gesellschaftsschicht, welcher um die Jahrhundertwende in breiten Kreisen Beliebtheit genoss. Man war von Ideologien und Theorien unbeschwert; man sah, wie Vaughan Williams formulierte, 'das Elend von Reichtum und Armut' in der Gesellschaft, und man zielte darauf, das Los der Unterdrückten zu verbessern, ohne jedoch die bestehende Gesellschaftsordnung umwälzen zu wollen. Die Form von Sozialismus war ernst gemeint und ernstzunehmen, half sie doch tatsächlich mit, in diesem Jahrhundert die wirtschaftliche Lage der Arbeiter Englands zu verbessern. Und im Falle der erwähnten Komponisten erlaubte gerade die Passivität dieses Sozialismus dessen Umsetzung in jene Art von Musikästhetik, wie sie bei Vaughan Williams zum Ausdruck kommt, nämlich, dass der Künstler seiner Gesellschaft dienen, und mit seiner Musik das Gemeinwohl propagieren solle. Er gehört also nicht zu einer Elite, darf sich nicht von seinem Publikum abkapseln. Wenn er die Stimme seines Publikums nicht mehr hört, kann er nicht mehr hoffen, seine Kunst zum Ausdruck der Gesellschaft zu machen..." (WALTON 1994:262-264).

"Vaughan Williams was, as were Holst, Britten, and also Tippett, a follower of that Victorian, paternalistic socialism of the upper class that enjoyed widespread popularity around the turn of the century. One was free from ideologies and theories; one saw, as Vaughan Williams stated, 'the misery of wealth and poverty' in society, and one aimed to improve the lot of the suppressed without wanting to roll, nevertheless, over the existing social order. This form of socialism was meant seriously and was taken seriously; nevertheless, it really helped to improve the economic position of workers in England in this century. And, in the case of the above-mentioned composers, just the passiveness of this socialism permitted its conversion into that kind of musical aesthetic that is expressed by Vaughan Williams, namely that the artist is a servant of society, and he shall use his music to propagate the public will. He does not belong to an élite, may not isolate himself from his audience. If he does not hear the voice of his audience any-more, he can no longer hope to make his art the expression of society...")

Although Walton is quoting the generation of composers preceding Arnold in order to prove his thesis, Arnold's political position and his close ties to Communist ideals are testified (HARRIS/MEREDITH 2004:228-230). Furthermore, he felt close to the English labour union movement, which was clearly based on Socialist ideals. He received a commission from the Trade Union Congress (TUC) to compose the *Peterloo Overture, opus 97*.[74] The fact that Arnold also apparently earned a lot of money from royalties generated by his film music, making him the richest capitalist composer in England, reveals the conflict that Arnold experienced as a composer and as a person. Being a servant to an audience, as Vaughan Williams was, and identifying himself in that way ("...When I am asked to write music for a ballet, a school orchestra, a film or a revue, I write exactly what I would like to hear if I were to go to the particular entertainment for which the music has been commissioned. On quite a number of occasions my ideas have coincided with other people's – from which you will gather that my stars have been lucky indeed! [ARNOLD 1956:169]), his Communist and Socialist outlook is inconsistent in this respect, as it does not reflect the reality of a composer who understands his occupation as a passion requiring appropriate remuneration in order to maintain his lifestyle. Arnold understands his "occupation" in a professional context, being able to compose any work at any time, even it is just music for a TV advertisement.[75] However, is Saremba's reproach that Arnold would have written works for a concert room just from pure *plaisir* (quoted at the beginning of this study) really justifiable?

Aside from the "genius myth", an artist's occupation, in particular that of the composer, is prescribed by another concept: l'art pour l'art. In order to create a true piece of art the artist must supposedly focus on personal strivings and the act of creating, without regard for monetary interests. Many people still cling to this image of a "good" or "true" composer who idealistically pursues his art, is poor, and is often daring in character. A financially successful composer, conversely, is treated with caution and viewed through resentful eyes.

Nevertheless, this simplification leads to the wrong conclusion that financially successful composers can only be found within the circles of light music – one may remind oneself again of Adorno acting as an extreme critic of film music in general. Nowadays, fortunately, Adorno's criticism has been joined by criticism of Adorno himself[76] – but, certainly, the ostensible professionalism and routine enabling of a composer of light music to create works as insatiably as a caterpillar has hardly anything to do with the image of composers of a more serious genre.

---

[74] The description of the premiere is found in Harris and Meredith's book (HARRIS/MEREDITH 2004:264f).

[75] We have Paul Harris to thank for the *Theme for Players*, music for a John Player TV commercial, Queen's Temple Publications, QT173.

[76] The already mentioned author Christine Eichel shall play principal witness again: „....Die Musikästhetik Th. W. Adornos hat hier den Stellenwert eines heuristischen Schlüssels, weil sie eine Doppelfigur im Umgang mit Klischees beschreibt.Adorno kämpft gegen Klischees - gedanklich, sprachlich, werktheoretisch. Doch gleichzeitig wurde Adorno selbst zum Opfer eines Klischees: als vermeintlicher Kronzeuge eines rigiden und zunehmenden blinden Modernismus..." (Eichel 1994:161). ("... *The musical aesthetics of Th. W. Adorno represent a heuristic clef because he presents a double-sided figure with regard to stereotypes. Adorno fights against stereotypes – in his thoughts, in his writings, theoretically. However, at the same time Adorno himself became the victim of a stereotype: as a putative principal witness of a rigid and increasingly blind modernism...*")

4. British Contemporary Music: Classical Thinking, Progress, Musical Life, the Market Economy, the General Public, and Aesthetic Categorisation within the British Modern Age: The Construction of Arnold's Image

If Arnold has often been the victim of such attacks, now we shall have a closer look at another British representative of the composer's curia – but not with the intention of maligning his excellent compositional quality. But understanding the real life of a composer, understanding the triad of the audience, the publisher's interests, and compositional independence, will help to provide a more comprehensive image of Arnold and will hopefully revise the idea that Arnold composed primarily for profit. Drum roll for: Benjamin Britten!

The British musicologist Paul Kildea wrote a notable study, published in 2002, which he gave the equivocal title, *Selling Britten*. He claims that Benjamin Britten's success as a composer was possible only due to a confluence of several different factors. He does not question the high quality of Benjamin Britten's works, nor does he question the frenzied acceptance of his audience.[77] Instead, he examines the connections between the composer, the British Arts Council, the BBC, and Britten's publishers, Boosey and Hawkes and Oxford University Press, as well as the special market situation of contemporary music in Great Britain.

Kildea first posits that Benjamin Britten clearly understood all of these connections very early on. His professionalism in understanding all of these factors and drawing the appropriate conclusions from them meant that the public in Great Britain was able to perceive his unquestionably high compositional quality. If Kildea's argument that Britten understood, early on, the importance of the development of the long-playing record industry (KILDEA 2002:4) may initially seem naïve, in a burgeoning media-oriented society filled with broadcasting companies, book and music publishing houses, and television, Britten recognises the inescapable power of market conditions. In order for any work be played for the first time by the BBC, the full score had to be submitted to a committee at the broadcasting-company and to the panel of the music division of the BBC (GARNHAM 2003:137). If it was then considered for broadcasting, the proper performance materials (parts, scores) were required – could it be that a professional score layout, nicely typed, and the support of a prestigious and excellent publisher were of help?[78] Britten, as a young composer, was not at all surprised by these developments in mass media, and recognised their advantages. Being first in the chain of the media system, he then tried to develop his role, and affect the system from within by establishing the Aldeburgh festivals[79] in 1948.

"...Where other musicians spoke of the disastrous consequences of change, Britten quickly established relationships with the agents of change. The first of these was with publishing – a prerequisite for any *professional* composer...In the same period, Britten began exploring wider markets, via the BBC...

The Aldeburgh Festival, established in 1948, increasingly became the principal forum for Britten premieres. As with the EOG (English Opera Group),

---

[77] The BBC music journalist and pupil of Schoenberg, Hans Keller, belonged not only to Benjamin Britten's circle of friends, but can be regarded as one of the most important protégés of Britten's music. In this context, *cf.* Garnham's statements (GARNHAM 2003:17-19).

[78] Kildea summarises: "...*A Boy Was Born* illustrated one less obvious but fundamentally important feature of the BBC's programming: composers either had to produce scores and parts themselves, or pay for their production by professional copyists. Either expense or timescale, therefore, could militate against the performance of new generous scale work. And it is clear that Britten came to see this in the 1930s as a vital point..." (KILDEA 2002:47).

[79] Kildea is even not afraid to label Britten as "Aldeburgh's Court Composer" – indeed, the dominance of Britten's compositions is a striking argument: "...The change in Britten's compositional priorities was quite obviously progressive...only four of the seventeen works from the 1950s with an opus number were first presented at Aldeburgh; in the 1960s two-thirds of those pieces with Britten's imprimatur were premiered at a festival" (KILDEA 2002:180).

economic parameters shaped the product...In the 1960s Britten retreated to Aldeburgh and new supply patterns developed: music was premiered at the Festival, broadcast by the BBC, published by Boosey & Hawkes or the new Faber Music, recorded by Decca, and quickly put on the market...

Britten was, therefore, a modern, professional composer..." (KILDEA 2002:4-5).

Even if one emphasises the existence of letters between the publisher, editor, and composer, which reveal that Britten did not even hesitate to transpose pieces for choir or vocal a major second down because of better marketing possibilities (KILDEA 2002:14-16), the image of Benjamin Britten as a modern and professional composer, does not, as already noted, detract from his compositional achievements. Rather, a positive trait becomes evident. Britten realistically understood the occupational nature of a composer, did not attempt to lock himself in an ivory tower, and was therefore able to relate to the desires of his audience, giving them a gift in the form of music that they valued. One of his true achievements, was his ablity to understand the style of music that was popular in Great Britain in 1945 and during the following decades, and to do so in his own professionally organised – let's call it "managed" – way.

In comparing Britten's development to Arnold's, a remarkable common characteristic comes to light. Arnold's music was integrated during the fifties into a comparable media compound system, as was Britten's. The frequent performances of Arnold's works, his Oscar for best soundtrack (1957), and the huge popular success of his works that were performed at cartoonist and artist Gerald Hoffnung's festivals in 1956-1961 clearly underscores that. Still, as simple as the statement may sound, Arnold is not Britten and Britten is not Arnold.

The author's point of view is as follows: Saremba's reproach was unwarranted. Saremba pursued, as many annotators and commentators have, the path of least resistance – dismissing the idea of examining Arnold's characteristics and stating that Arnold was unique, rather than representative. Even if Chris Walton's four theses offer an easy solution to the British enigma overall, they still cannot be applied to Arnold.

Hence, the author proposes the following thesis. Let's accept that Arnold's compositional virtuosity manifests itself in a style that is initially influenced by more traditional and more conservative poles (Sibelius, Mahler, Berlioz). However, he then develops a personal style that does not measure compositional quality purely as progress in aesthetic categories, but represents a style in which the choice and means of compositional expression is truly free. He exhibits perfect, polished, clear orchestration skills that include all the achievements of the symphonic romantic tradition, as well as contemporary music techniques at the highest level of serious music as art. A piece of art which, as intended by the composer, also draws on popular music – jazz, *salon* music, pop[80] – e.g., from a non-artificial source, can always be justified by the composer simply because he **wanted** it to be that way. Arnold was a composer whose work is diverse, varied, multifaceted; a composer who appeared in the morning as

---

[80] Malcolm Arnold was not afraid to orchestrate John Lord's symphony for a rock band (Deep Purple) and a symphony orchestra, or to conduct it, either.

Shostakovitch's friend and at night as an admirer of jazz trumpeter Louis Armstrong. But, sadly, in reality he was a composer who did not understand why the music world, which was not able to categorise him, made his life so difficult and who, as a result, made his own life difficult. The list of Arnold's unique qualities could be continued ad infinitum, but only his music itself truly speaks to what makes Arnold unique in British contemporary music. Therefore, two works, which have much in common musically and compositionally, shall now be analysed: *A Grand, Grand Festival Overture, opus 57* (1956) and the second movement of his *Symphony No. 4, opus 71, vivace ma non troppo* (1960).

A Grand, Grand Festival Overture was composed in 1956 as Arnold's main contribution to the first Gerald Hoffnung Festival.[81] What is especially apparent in his composition, aside from the normative full symphonic orchestra apparatus, is the use of unusual solo instruments. Three vacuum cleaners, four floor polishers, and four rifles appear as soloists. While these soloists are hardly used thematically – their appearance could rather be called humorous – the following analysis will direct its attention towards the structure of the composition as well as towards the principal subject.

The structure of the composition is simple (*cf.* excursion); formal divisions can be drawn more or less schematically at the starting points of the respective rehearsal letters. Because of the use of returning sections, the composition itself could also be regarded as rondo-like, although in this interpretation it cannot be determined which of the several sections *is* the actual rondo subject. On the other hand, the most likely section to be called the rondo subject appears only later in the development. From letter N on, a strong parallelism is given to the introduction; therefore, it should be spoken of in terms of repetitive structures within a regular concert overture.

For the first time, at F, Arnold confronts us with a lyrical subject that is now perceived, in contrast to the already-presented chord arpeggios or fanfare-like motifs, as a thematic idea. Its basis is an example of effectiveness and simplicity. The subject, composed in a simple antecedent-consequent structure,[82] sprays the charm of a child-like melody – and this equally is its point. It remains omnipresent to the listener; it is – colloquially formulated – a catchy tune that is further harmonised in a simple way. Indeed, the rhythmical syncopation, first appearing in the accompanying chords in the strings, creates a counterpole to the melody of the woodwinds (flutes/oboes); however, this is a compositional method that cannot be described as artificial. Nevertheless, Arnold's compositional

---

[81] Regarding the history of this festival and Arnold's, *cf.* Cole, Jackson, and Harris/Meredith (COLE 1989:122-124; JACKSON 2003:79-81; HARRIS/MEREDITH 2004:149-157).
[82] However, the consequent is extended by two bars; therefore, it is compounded of 8 plus 10 bars.

trick of orchestrating this principal subject[83] in a transparent orchestration – in contrast to the grandiose-seeming fanfares – is ingenious. The fact that he applies it **economically** and only at well-chosen places ([F], [G], [J], [P], [Q],[84] [S]) underlines that, too. It prevents the listener from becoming bored, and the stereotypes of an overture are equally qualified. However, the subject, having already been recognised in the beginning, increases the qualification in a formal sense, too. What is rare is perceived as special.

---

[83] The lyrical subject shall be called the "principal subject". This conclusion is obvious because of its singular appearance and its important position within the development of the composition.
[84] In [Q], only fragments of the subject are quoted.

A Grand, Grand Festival Overture

Malcolm Arnold

Figure 20 *A Grand, Grand Festival Overture*, **excerpt from letter** $\boxed{F}$ **on; transcribed by the author**

A Grand, Grand Overture, op. 57
Music by Malcolm Arnold
© Copyright 1956 Paterson's Publication Limited
All Rights Reserved. International Copyright Secured.
Reproduced by permission.

It is a pity that, in the scientific literature published so far, the use of non-orchestral instruments in *A Grand, Grand Festival Overture* is often overemphasised. Thus, the overture, only eight minutes long, can be thought of more as a regular concert overture with added vacuum-cleaner passages. The beginning brass-section motif, with two quavers (G flat and B flat), is answered by humorous pizzicatos, as in G flat and B flat, only in crotchets. The B-flat major scale, outlined in the strings from letter $\boxed{A}$, leads to a sustained B-flat major chord. A lonely piccolo flute states quick chord figurations in semiquavers; the chord used is an E-major chord with an added major seventh. Again, a polytonal tension is created, B-flat major against E major. This pattern of dissolving polytonal harmony by the use of chord arpeggios belongs, by the way, to Arnold's preferred composition method and is also found in *Concerto for Trumpet and Orchestra*, opus 125, composed in 1982. In the trumpet concerto, the solo trumpet plays fanfare-like B-flat major motifs while the strings arpeggiate an E-major chord in countermotion, but this relation is exactly in reverse in the Festival Overture between the strings and the solo piccolo flute (*cf.* both illustrations).

Figure 21 *Concerto for Trumpet and Orchestra*, beginning of third movement: B-flat major/E major polytonality

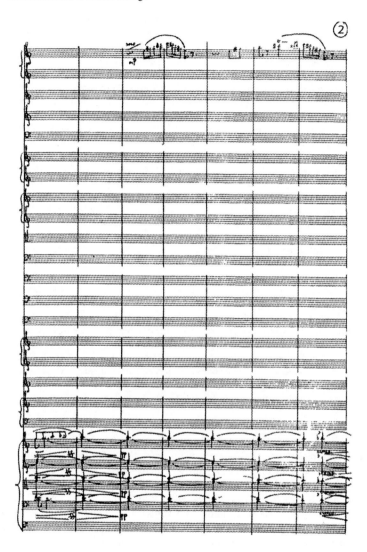

Figure 22 *A Grand, Grand Festival Overture*, **excerpt of full score, b. 8-14, polytonality**

A Grand, Grand Overture, op. 57
Music by Malcolm Arnold
© Copyright 1956 Paterson's Publication Limited
All Rights Reserved. International Copyright Secured.
Reproduced by permission.

The work is dominated by fast scale "runs", countless fanfare motifs and quizzical motifs (especially Ⓛ), the woodwinds executing a quaver motif aped by the strings in the notion of goats). It ends in a final chord battle, recreating the mood of the fourth movement of Beethoven's 1st Symphony, but exceeding this in its pungency. The amount of the Hoover vacuum cleaners, "tuned" to three different pitches (high-medium-low), is only 100 bars out of the total of 429 bars of the full composition. Three vacuum cleaners start, generally, consecutively and form, therefore, nothing other than a sort-of three-part texture chord, whose sound frames are determined statically, showing no internal fluctuation. Jackson summarises, referring to another work by Arnold for toy piano, "Like the vacuum cleaners and floor polishers in the *Grand, Grand Overture*, Arnolds treats the...instruments with respect. At no time do we feel that he is making fun of them" (JACKSON 2003:81), but this judgement sounds cursory. The vacuum cleaners enter on their own; nevertheless they reveal no musically thematic relationship to the musical material of the work. They form an interesting sound texture. Jackson neglects musicological and music-theoretical analysis, ignoring the question of whether an element is necessary or to what extent its use is logically derived. Jackson appears to have been influenced by his own personal taste, and his analysis pays too much tribute to it.

Still, *A Grand, Grand Festival Overture*, revealing a miniaturistic structure and a musical vitality, humour, and irony – once more one is reminded of the absurd chord battle – can be regarded as part of the genre of works for "special occasions" (COLE 1989:122). Further, analysis should focus on the fact that Arnold tends to use idiomatic musical languages from the worlds of functional music and serious music, but in point of fact, Arnold does not think in these categories at all. Arnold without humour is not the Arnold who is able to simultaneously express the highest elation, depression, or even melancholy in his works, no matter whether they were written for the concert room or simply for plaisir. Arnold's vocabulary is ambiguous and seemingly unlimited. Above all, he does not reject any musical language out of hand. If he is attracted to a certain idiom, he immediately integrates it into his style. Let us state it more directly: Arnold constantly extends his vocabulary.

Let us now look at Arnold's 4th Symphony. First, it should be emphasised that while both the 4th and *A Grand, Grand Festival Overture* were commissioned works, they were intended for different types of audiences and in this respect they differ from each other. In the case of the 4th Symphony, for example, not only the general public but also the professionals were purposefully addressed. The work itself was commissioned by the BBC under the aegis of its Controller of Music, William Glock.[85] It premiered in November 1960, played by the BBC Symphony Orchestra and conducted by the composer. It holds a central position among Arnold's complete works because it was written after years of commercial work. Between 1957 and 1960 Arnold wrote 13 film soundtracks, including his most famous ones, *The Bridge on the River Kwai* and *The Inn of the Sixth Happiness*, as well as works for special occasions (*A Grand, Grand Festival Overture, opus 57, The Commonwealth Christmas Overture, opus 64*, and *The United Nations*, for four military bands, organ, and orchestra). Arnold then once again devoted himself fully to symphonic writing.[86]

---

[85] That Glock was the promoter cannot be directly proven.
[86] The 3rd Symphony, opus 63, was composed in 1957.

Harris/Meredith have touched only very cursorily on Arnold's musical structure, instead primarily questioning to what extent Arnold deals with the race riots of Notting Hill through his use of Caribbean instruments in the percussion section, assuming that Arnold was delivering a quasi-political statement (HARRIS/MEREDITH 2004:190 et seqq.). Cole and Jackson, however, (COLE 1989:106 et seqq.) (JACKSON 2003:99 et seqq.) have more precisely examined the musical structure of the eight-bar subject in the second movement, which Jackson calls a "trio" (JACKSON 2003:101). They have also pointed out its palindrome structure, although Jackson has more or less copied Cole's theses by paraphrasing them.

Figure 23 The Idea of Subject: 4ᵗʰ Symphony, second movement, clearly deduced palindrome structure[87]

Symphony No. 4, op. 71
Music by Malcolm Arnold
© Copyright 1960 Paterson's Publication Limited.
All Rights Reserved. International Copyright Secured.
Reproduced by Permission

Indeed, the palindrome structure can be recognised very easily – the idea of an accidental origin can in fact be excluded. Arnold generates a dance-like and extremely humorous character, particularly from letter F on, where the subject first appears in the clarinet while the strings are creating rhythmical counterpoles through their pizzicato chords, each of them placed on different beats. This can be seen in particular from bar six on. Nevertheless, Arnold's very sophisticated instrumentation, the palindromic structure of the subject, and, above all, the overall texture (one could also use the concept of "manner of speaking") must not mislead us about the fact that the real, basic structure of the subject is simple. It is a

---

[87] Illustration from Cole (COLE 1989:109).

4. British Contemporary Music: Classical Thinking, Progress, Musical Life, the Market
Economy, the General Public, and Aesthetic Categorisation within the British Modern Age:
The Construction of Arnold's Image

simple antecedent-consequent structure, divided into 2+2+4,[88] and is
therefore structurally similar to the subject of *A Grand, Grand Festival
Overture*.

Arnold devotes himself exclusively to this idea in the following
sections. The following 64 bars can be deduced exclusively from this
material, and only from letter O does he start to use the material substance
from the very beginning of the movement, which can be called its real
essence in this respect.[89] This material is used for two purposes. First, it
leads **in** and **out** of the subject. Second, it is of enormous importance for
the function and the course of the movement. In addition, it is subjected to
more advanced compositional procedures.

Arnold begins the second movement with a sort-of "film of
lubricant": based on the melodic B-flat minor scale, the notes B flat, C, D
flat, E flat, F, G flat, and A flat enter consecutively, scored to con sordino
strings, and remain as a pad. An additional B flat, softly pushed by the
trombones, creates the notion of a tonic, which is disturbed, however, in
bar 4 by the note A, scored in octave unisons in contrabassoon, tuba,
kettledrum, and pizzicato cellos and basses. To make this indifferent
texture even more harmonically bewildering, a triadic staccato figuration
in bar 8 is applied by the piccolo. Nevertheless, from bar 9 on, the *Gestalt*
of this figuration almost evokes the notion of a sort of cadence – at least
such an impression is outlined. On beat 4 in bar 9, an ascending clarinet
run is added, based upon the scale notes of the string pad texture. This run
is repeated by the first flute and almost quizzically answered by the
clarinets (bar 11 et seqq.). It is emphasised as a triumvirate by another
element, two minor thirds textures, stratified to each other and scored as
pizzicato strings.[90] The latter steer attention away from the centrality of the
bass note A.

---

[88] I would like to separate the last four bars. The following two bars do not correspond to each
other, but instead outline one single thought that is only finished in the final (ninth) bar. This
bar is also overlapped with the statement of the subject, now in the oboe, *cf.* letter G.
[89] In a mathematical respect, these parts predominate, while the thematic idea is limited, as
described, to 64 bars.
[90] We could also conclude an F-minor seventh chord with added minor ninth and omitted fifth,
appearing in a quaver. However, because of the interplay between the thirds (four bars before
letter A), I prefer the interpretation of two third structures complementing each other.

4. British Contemporary Music: Classical Thinking, Progress, Musical Life, the Market
Economy, the General Public, and Aesthetic Categorisation within the British Modern Age:
The Construction of Arnold's Image

II

Figure 24 4th Symphony, second movement, pages 1 and 2

Symphony No. 4, op. 71
Music by Malcolm Arnold
© Copyright 1960 Paterson's Publication Limited.
All Rights Reserved. International Copyright Secured.
Reproduced by Permission

Two moments are of particular importance in this analysis. First, the resemblance to *A Grand, Grand Festival Overture* is remarkable, wherein a chord texture – indeed, substantially of a more consonant character – in the strings is also contrasted with a vital piccolo flute figuration. Second, the interplay of these three elements (piccolo staccato figuration, scale runs, and the consecutive chain of thirds) determines Arnold's compositional technique up to the letter $\boxed{F}$, i.e., until the appearance of the thematic idea in A minor. Arnold knows, in a very skillful way, not to wear out these three elements, instead emphasising them through mutations, variations, or easier compositional procedures. Note, for example, the augmentation of the piccolo figuration, taken from section $\boxed{B}$ to create a relationship with the beginning, or the canonical structure between the first trombone and the bassoon/contrabasses at letter $\boxed{C}$. Let us therefore ask a few heretical questions: Why does Arnold actually introduce the thematic idea in A minor – indeed, in its effect extremely gallant and joking – if he returns – after 64 bars – to the initial elements? Why does he then differentiate these elements with uncanny exactness?[91] Is he a victim of the classical trio form (ABA), apparently very reactionary for the early sixties, and does his use of this form force him to approach it in this way? Or, has he become a victim of his habit to equip every composition with a "good tune"?

To find a solution, we need to carefully examine the transitional situation just before letter $\boxed{F}$. In contrast to the preceding development, revealing an *Ineinanderverschränkung* of the three described elements, Arnold tries purposely to construct a bridge (transition) by means of different structural levels, eight bars before letter $\boxed{F}$. The use of the kettledrum shall be regarded as level 1: while the kettledrum is still playing the bass note E in $\boxed{E}$, the note is changed during the last eight bars before $\boxed{F}$ to A, repeated monotonously on the fourth beat of a 6/8 – although the whole harmonic context does not point at all to A in this section. At the moment of the transition to the new thematic idea (the subject), the A tonality had really already been established as a frame. Arnold acts very smartly here: he does not consciously repeat the kettledrum at the beginning of $\boxed{F}$, leading to the fact that the listener's expectation is not fulfilled. The entry of the clarinet, marked *piano*, is thus covered on beat 1 by the A-minor triad of the strings, which provides an echo effect. This procedure almost creates the notion of a new colour of tonality; it is remarkable how specifically Arnold combines instrumentation and overall structure at this point.

The second level concerns the augmented form of the staccato figuration. Arnold quotes the beginning; however, this infers – and this is to be called the third level – with a new layer. In the strings, he adds a harmonic ostinato, changing its chord each dotted crotchet. On the one hand, the chords themselves create an effect that has not yet been used, stressing the degree of dissonance and its dissonant inside intervals. On the other hand, the fact that the chord ostinato consists of three successive chords leads to a *Verschränkung* of chords in terms of chord-change

---

[91] *cf.* the staccato figuration idea from letter $\boxed{P}$ on, comparable to Webern's transparency and pointillism.

frequency. In each 6/8 bar, only two chord changes take place; therefore, the ostinato appears altogether only five times in its complete form; the sixth time, it is not stated completely, *cf.* letter F. This approach clearly indicates Arnold's compositional formula: big differences are often created using only marginalities.

Figure 25 4th Symphony, letters F and G

Arnold has created a powerful transition section, directly leading into the following palindromic thematic idea. Nevertheless, the impression remains that Arnold could have progressed through the development section in a more classical sense (as in the case of *A Grand, Grand Festival Overture*). In that way, the strengths of the thematic material, constructed of both superficial simplicity and concurrent complexity (palindrome), could have been presented much more in the foreground.

Christopher Stasiak states that part of the four movements of the 4th Symphony suffers from the following problem:...Passages are often repeated direct, with little or no change to their fundamental outline, and do not always move far away from their original key centres; combined with their sectional nature, this hinders their ability to work as passages of development within the symphonic context..." (STASIAK 1987:87). The actual frequent literal or marginal change on another tonic indeed intensifies the experience of the thematic material, but at the same time limits the possibilities of creating an extensive symphonic development. However, to qualify this statement, one must confess that Stasiak's analysis of the 4th Symphony (a published essay in 1987), deals with all of Arnold's symphonies.[92] In addition, it only consists of one short paragraph and therefore cannot be deep enough. The judgement, later stated by Stasiak, that "...The one exception is the finale. This follows the successful formula of the finale of the First Symphony, having a fugal (which gives it a sense of purposeful activity) leading on to an Alla Marcia that heralds the closing passage of music..." (STASIAK 1987:87), should also be critically discussed. In the final movement, a plausible end can easily be created by vitality (with quicker tempos, like con fuoco) or by typical phrases (fanfares, strokes, sustained chords, tremolos on the kettledrums, etc.). This is in contrast to a middle movement.

Nevertheless, Stasiak's criticism is formulated without value, as opposed to other contemporary annotators; Porter's criticism of the premiere already reveals certain "abusive" features: "...Malcolm Arnold's Fourth is a symphony for fun, written almost in defiance, it would seem...Assuming that it is meant seriously...then it must be... intended as a challenge. Arnold has settled for popular idioms of our day, gone to the ballrooms a first movement part Edmundo Ros, part Victor Sylvester, with a second theme that needs only 'lyrics' to be a palais pop. The Scherzo is a perky, ingenious reworking of the theme of the seventh English Dance. There is a lushly romantic Andantino...and a Finale which strikingly recalls the *Young Person's Guide*, and also includes a rumbustious march, Mahlerian and *Alexander's Rag Time Band* at once. The Symphony is exuberant, melodious, unabashed, likeable – and written with all Arnold's wonted skill. And after all it was the Devil who spoilt man's fun by whispering: 'But is it Art'?" (PORTER 1960:766).

Can we agree with Porter in this respect or are these only prejudices from his own recollection?

---

[92] The ninth was not included because it had not yet been written.

English Dances, Set II, 7. Satz

Malcolm Arnold

Figure 26 *English Dances, Set II, opus 33*, **seventh movement, grazioso**

Reproduced by permission Alfred Lengnick & Co Ltd.

Indeed, the subject of the seventh movement of the English Dances, Set II shows resemblances to the 4th symphony, however: Porter's analysis ignores first of all that the thematic material is used in another context, and also that the subject of the second movement of the 4th Symphony is "worked" much more in its rhythmical substance. While in the English Dances the context can be described as sustained chords of dotted quaver-duration, supported later by a quaver figuration of harp and celesta (see letter [C]), leading to the impression of a full orchestral landscape, in the 4th symphony, the "oddness" of the orchestration and the use of syncopation are the main factors. Porter has cursorily discovered a relationship. It is a pity, however, that he does not look at it from an analytic point of view, instead preferring the easy way out of criticising it by providing flimsy evidence.

Nevertheless, Arnold does repeat himself in a certain way; this repetition interestingly appears only in his late oeuvre and is never absolutely literal. Comparing likewise the subjects of two other dances, the third movement (piacevole) from the Four Irish Dances, opus 126 (1986) and the first movement of his Four Welsh Dances (1989), it becomes obvious that sequence patterns are used in both. In the latter, though, the influence of chromaticism is much less, and the melody seems weakened by the use of a more diatonic structure – but the melodic contour of both subjects is very similar. Special attention should be paid now to the top note A of the Welsh Dances, particular in bar 3. Arnold focuses on this note in such a repetitive way that the note, at first creating tension, loses this attribute and is neutralised by the repetition of the octave. Furthermore, in bar 7, the clear differences between both subjects can be recognised. The triadic arpeggio is there contrasted with dotted minims, acting as harmonic suspensions (see illustration). Also, the phrasing clearly differs.

Themengegenüberstellung Welsh/Irish Dances

Malcolm Arnold

Figure 27 Subjects of *Four Irish Dances* versus *Four Welsh Dances*

Four Irish Dances, opus 126 © Faber Music Ltd.
Reproduced by permission. All rights reserved.
Four Welsh Dances, op. 138
Music by Malcolm Arnold
© Copyright 1989 Orpheus Publications.
© Copyright Assigned 1989 to Novello & Company Limited.
All Rights Reserved. International Copyright Secured.
Reproduced by Permission.

A completely different orchestration is applied here by Arnold. In contrast to the scanty scoring for strings in the Irish Dances, in which beat 2 is emphasised in the first two bars, he elaborates his orchestration in the Welsh Dances by creating a more colourful image. The main melody is played in unison by the first flute as well as the glockenspiel and the harp, while the first violins and violas supply a harmonic background, replaced from bar 4 onward by the low string section. If this effect is hidden in the score, becoming almost insignificant, the change of sound is, in contrast, clearly audible and recognisable.

Figure 28 *Four Welsh Dances, opus 138*, **first movement (excerpt)**

Four Welsh Dances, op. 138
Music by Malcolm Arnold
© Copyright 1989 Orpheus Publications.
© Copyright Assigned 1989 to Novello & Company Limited.
All Rights Reserved. International Copyright Secured.
Reproduced by Permission.

Figure 29 *Four Irish Dances, opus 126,* third movement (excerpt)

The fact that Arnold creates in the second movement of his 4th Symphony an extremely simple subject, easily memorable should not lead to misinterpretation. Instead, the question of whether or not the mixing of two hemispheres – the three levels and their complicated symphonic elaboration versus the simplicity[93] of the thematic idea from which a soundtrack or a pop song could have been composed – hinders him from realising his initial claims of a real symphonic development should be stressed.

Arnold has clearly confessed two points of view in his essay "I think of music in terms of sound", published in 1956 and often discussed among the public. On the one hand, a composer should always consider the actual instrumentalists in the orchestra; on the other hand, he should never lose the idea of development within a piece of composition. "...Another point which is always in my mind is that of development. If one is *really* honest in listening to the music of all periods there are times when one's mind is inclined to wander...To put it crudely, the mind wanders during the sections that occur in music between the recognisable themes – always assuming that the theme or themes have said something to the listener.

Very, very roughly speaking, these parts of composition are usually development sections; one cannot write a piece of music by just repeating one theme, unless it is a special effort one is after as in Ravel's *Bolero*. A composer has to compose something after contrasts and will show his original thought in a new light, and the play between these two or three or even more thoughts goes to make up a composition..." (ARNOLD 1956:167).

It is astonishing how strongly the musical analysis of the second movement of Arnold's 4th Symphony has portrayed his aesthetic position concerning his own composition process. If Arnold really reveals that the mind of the listener goes wandering through the sections of a composition,

---

[93] Simplicity here as a judgement without value and prejudice...

and if we also consider his evaluation of the concept of recognisable themes, this really makes the following point very clear. Arnold confronts us therefore in the second movement with his own process of consideration between the symmetrical outside parts (based on the three mentioned structures) and the thematic idea, showing almost monothematic features in its deliberate repetitive character. He asks the listener to take part in this "...play between these two or three or even more thoughts". Stasiak's criticism of this procedure can be understood, however, in the understanding that Arnold's original intention loses its sharpness. The second movement suffers, if generally (*Pace* Stasiak!), from the following problem. The causal logic within the music, operating with the classicist idea of form,[94] lets us expect a stringent and above all chronological development from the composer's thoughts. The fact that Arnold uses the thematic idea **only** in the middle of the movement and then, instead of developing it, repeats it more or less literally, is cheeky but brilliant. Maybe he has been aiming for a kind of Bolero effect in the sense of a *stylus Ravelus* – however, this may be pure speculation.

The same compositional techniques are applied in large parts of *A Grand, Grand Festival Overture*. We should not misinterpret this, and, by reviewing these two works, should not establish a general rule in the case of Arnold's complete works. In his compositional technique, he is able to follow all current and **typical** development techniques, corresponding therefore to the expectations of causal-logical development. Nevertheless, at the end of the fifties, Arnold's tendency to negate this becomes obvious. However, if he needs these techniques, he again uses his vocabulary – and how impressively he uses this vocabulary shall be pointed out within the scope of the analysis of his 6th Symphony (*cf.* the author's analytic and music-theoretical statements).

The typical music criticism of the sixties and early seventies mainly confronted continental-European composers aiming for the rejection of archetypal classical form models, but the BBC also played a fateful role in Arnold's case. The BBC, faced not only with a programmatic but also a personnel break (*cf.* Hans Keller retiring from the BBC in 1960) during the sixties, were at least partially responsible for the increasing isolation of Arnold – even if this must be evaluated in the context of this particular time. In this respect, Burton-Page is right when he describes this as a "...sea-change in the Corporation's attitude to living British composers, a change that was not necessarily going to operate in Malcolm Arnold's favour..."[95] (BURTON-PAGE 1994:116-119).

---

[94] Ligeti's *Atmosphères* is a counterexample. Arch-shaped structures play a vital role – for example, the parameter of the textural density takes over the function to indicate stages of development.

[95] Garnham (especially) has pointed out the BBC's change and the adjustment towards an avant-garde and much more contemporary style of music, accompanied by the appointment of William Glock as the new Controller of Music in 1959. He also shows how closely Glock and Keller co-operated at first and that only later did they become diametrical opposites due to their personal musical preferences (GARNHAM 2003:79;81;88-89;90;137).

If we now summarise the present results: What do *A Grand, Grand Festival Overture* and *Symphony No. 4* have in common, how do they differ, and how can these results help to position Arnold within the context of British contemporary music?

First, a basic feature of Arnold's composition process can be demonstrated quite strikingly with the help of both works. Indeed, Arnold spends a lot of time elaborating on the thematic material and the actual subject. However, the subject itself can usually be described as "simple" in its melodic contour and form. This would initially be a not unusual sign – think of the tendency found in the classical epoch where complex structures (as in the baroque) were more and more neglected in favour of simple textures. Thus, many symphonic works of the classical period distinguish themselves by the fact that their simple subjects are developed and realised in a highly advanced manner. With regard to Arnold, it was unusual that music critics and professionals tended to negate his ability to develop a piece of art from these thematic constellations. Remember Hans Keller's comments on Arnold's 2nd Symphony – if one considers them clearly, it becomes obvious that, even if not in every respect, much of the criticism was no more than repetition of a single image full of prejudices.

Second, music-theoretical analysis has clearly indicated the following: Arnold, technically versed as a composer, achieves a deliberate effect on the listener by using the easiest of compositional procedures. It is therefore his perfection, his mastery, his knowledge of these choices and of his means, and above all his control, that make Arnold one of the most discussed and isolated composers of the sixties, after having been prominent and popular in the fifties. Arnold's persistence in adhering to conventions and his belief in his very own personal style could also have evoked criticism –if it had been assessed by an unprejudiced music critic. There is no doubt about this. However, much of the past criticism fails to deeply acknowledge or classify his work, but reflects instead a lack of understanding among the public, who did not realise why Arnold continued to write in such a polystylistic manner. Moreover, there are clear signs of prejudice:

"...The four movements [of the Symphony] are well contrasted, the writing shows consistently the composer's consummate command of the orchestra...the work as a whole is unlikely to enhance Arnold's reputation since the invention is largely undistinguished and any element of novelty seems intended to stimulate the senses rather than to satisfy either the intellect or the spirit...Of the scherzo we are told 'This movement is not intended to arouse emotions that are necessarily pleasant', and in this negative aim it is undoubtedly successful for despite much ingenuity there is a conspicuous lack of piquancy and impetus, and this short movement suggests nothing so much as diluted and debased Prokofieff...This is not a valuable addition to British symphonic literature and does not show Arnold's undeniable genius to good advantage, but is, nevertheless, a remarkable tour de force, and we hope that when he writes his next symphony he will (a) do so as a result of inner compulsion as distinct from the consideration of a commission, and (b) by that time have sloughed [off]the contaminating influence of the cinema..." (C.G.-F. 1960:143-144)

Indeed, a conclusion would be too easy if here the general musical public was accused of not acknowledging Arnold and his work in such a manner as was due to him. But Arnold himself was inclined to treat the public gruffly, to make enemies within the BBC and elsewhere, and to fail to show enough respect toward authorities within the British system. He reacted bitterly to the harsh rejection of his music; unfortunately, he did not answer in what was considered a polite and "academically acceptable" manner. His answer, published in 1971 in the *Guardian*, only expressed his personal feelings (ARNOLD 1971:169 et seqq.).

Third, like no other British composer, Arnold is an example of the *Zwiespalt* between traditional and modern contemporary music and the inability to position composers within the scope of contemporary music.

These problems start with the concept "contemporary". Indeed, the age-old discussion about whether genuine "contemporary" music exists, in contrast to "old" music, may sound like the question of the chicken and the egg. It has been discussed not only during the ars nova, but also specifically in the twentieth century. A work is always a child of the times in which it was written. One might ask whether it would fit better in another epoch; however, the question can never be adequately resolved. Any answer would only be speculation. Even if Arnold had personally provided an answer during an interview, the risk of self-deception would still make it unreliable from a scientific point of view.

However, it is correct that, because of Arnold's constant production of new works, some works include more conventionalities than others do. Nowadays, the probability is statistically relatively high that all possible tonal combinations and textural combinations within the field of music have already been used by composers. Still, failing to question this supposition does not lead to any new insights.

The categorisation of Arnold as a composer, revealing what makes him unique within the scope of British music, leads to a core point. We must discuss the central issue of whether his works were influenced by tradition, or whether it is possible to describe his position as modern, or even postmodern.

Arnold's symphonic writing includes input from normative processes taken from the symphonic development of the eighteenth and nineteenth centuries: his preference for a main melody in the form of the already described concept tune, his clear conventional pattern of classical formal structures (rondo, sonata form, symmetrical forms, and palindromic forms like ABCBA), his preference for the diatonic toward chromaticism, and, if chromaticism is used, it is usually used to create a contrast with the diatonic and to point out its strengths (SCHAFER 1963:153). In spite of these conventionalities, Arnold's symphonic writing is in no way antique.. We would neither label Arnold *einen Wolf im Schafspelz* nor would we call him the new Mozart or Beethoven. His closeness to Mahler, Berlioz, and Sibelius, though, can be plausibly demonstrated. It is manifested in the narrative tone of his musical language and in the realisation of emotion (*cf.* second movement (lento) of the 2nd Symphony), and it is also impressively underscored by Arnold's inclination not to take things too seriously. His pointillistic humour in the final clauses of his symphonic works which critics called a "dull accessory", was in reality Arnold's strength. He knew how a symphony, a concert overture, or even the final clause of a chamber-music work should be professionally rounded out and concluded. The latter, however, cannot be applied in general to his works overall. The bright D-major chord in the last movement of his 9th Symphony[96] is not meant to be cheerful; rather, it represents hope and faith in a positive adjustment to life and music.

In terms of Arnold's aesthetics: it is, from a continental-European viewpoint, indeed enticing to dismiss Arnold because of the aesthetic writings coming either from the pen of Theodor Adorno or being *in petto* with the Frankfurt School. But the special situation of twentieth-century German music cannot be applied in any way to England. A comparison of the current aesthetic discussions about music at that time (1950) shows that the main focus was quite different in each country. While Adorno and his allegiance to Darmstadt dedicated themselves to the demarcation of existing artistic material and defined this process as a general credo, the premises in Great Britain were quite a different – underscored by the following statement by Hull in 1951. Hull is fully aware of the fact that a new generation was about to develop in Great Britain – and I would label Arnold as part of it – a generation united in its belief that advanced and more traditional ("reactionary") elements could be integrated within a single composition. However, as opposed to Germany, where composers such as Paul Hindemith and Carl Orff, in comparison to Stockhausen, Boulez, or even Henze, were seen as the "old guard", Hull stresses the positive features of this aesthetic. The simultaneous appearance of tonality in its old and new senses is striking: "...The composers now to be discussed are also 'forward-looking'...Their presence in the onward movement of our national music is due partly to the fact that the revolt against late romanticism has entered upon a second, consolidating phase...The situation is, rather, that Schönberg enriched the musical language with far-reaching resources which have become part of the expressive means available to later composers. Some of those within our group seem to have found that these resources are much to their purpose; others have evolved or turned to different means for their special needs; but every thoughtful composer of recent times has been compelled to decide his attitude towards this inheritance. A good deal of 'forward-looking' music tends rather than to strike a middle course between radical adherence to the major-minor key system, and unqualified loyalty to strictly equal treatment of the twelve notes in the chromatic scale. The effect is largely to reap the advantages of free tonality while permitting, so far as may be desirable, the near or remote implication of a key-centre. This

---

[96] *cf.* later statements by the author.

process, far from being reactionary, has proved a valuable step towards fuller yet disciplined liberty..." (HULL 1951:212 et seqq.).

It is therefore important to stress once again a basic difference between continental Europe and Great Britain. In the early fifties, the English did not consider it despicable to use conventionalities taken from the rich vocabulary of the past and allow them to culminate in a composer's unique personal style, resulting in the creation of **new contemporary** art. It was only from the mid-sixties on – a time when cultural institutions were looking for new faces and new, substantially younger composers than Arnold begin developing their own profiles – that mechanisms similar to those in post-war Germany took place.

Readers should be aware that the author does not intend to argue that there were no philosophical or aesthetic discussions in England after World War II – figures like Ludwig Wittgenstein or Karl Popper are weighty counterexamples. However, their focus lay in their philosophical attempts to describe *das Kunstwerk:* the piece of art itself. Phenomenological discussions were led on an abstract basis and did not (considering Adorno) pertain to composers personally.

It is interesting to look at another British representative, even if his research centres on quite a different field. Terry Eagleton (born in 1943 in Salford) is one of the most prolific figures of the British Cultural Theory movement. The author does not intend to offer a full presentation, since Eagleton's works represent great diversity of topic, brilliantly written, and often combined with the best of English humour and sarcasm. In *After Theory*, published in 2003 as a continuation of *The Illusions of Postmodernism* (1996), Eagleton critically questions the concepts of modernism and postmodernism and calls modernism a "cultural experiment" whose followers were still clearly based in traditionalism and often felt that they belonged to the classical bourgeoisie: "...Rimbaud, Picasso and Bertolt Brecht still had a classical bourgeoisie to be rude about. But its offspring, postmodernism, has not. It is just that it seems not to have noticed the fact, perhaps because it is too embarrassing to the classical bourgeoisie... It spends much of its time assailing absolute truth, objectivity, timeless moral values, scientific inquiry and a belief in historical progress. It calls into question the autonomy of the individual, inflexible social and sexual norms, and the belief that there are firm foundations to the world. Since all of these values belong to a bourgeois world on the wane, his is rather like firing off irascible letters to the press about the horse-riding Huns or marauding Carthaginians who have taken over the Home Counties..." (EAGLETON 2003:17).

Eagleton does not deny that modernism existed. But what modernism and postmodernism had in common was that they tried – in order to gain legitimacy – to rid themselves of conventional elements. A paradox was created in the case of postmodernism: in contrast to modernism, postmodernism was based on the idea of progress – but progress was considered a crime in and of itself.

"...Postmodernists reject the idea of progress because they are distracted by grand narratives. They assume that a belief in progress must entail that history as a whole has been steadily on the up from the outset, a view which they naturally dismiss as a delusion..." (EAGLETON 2003:179).

4. British Contemporary Music: Classical Thinking, Progress, Musical Life, the Market Economy, the General Public, and Aesthetic Categorisation within the British Modern Age: The Construction of Arnold's Image

How can Arnold be seen in light of Eagleton's statements? In spite of Arnold's Communist tendencies, he can – particularly for biographical purposes – be said to belong to the bourgeoisie, even if he was not born into this class. However, his whole persona is marked by the renown as a composer that he received from society, and the manner in which he attained it brought him both great joy and grief. The morality of this should not be questioned at all; not to mention that it is suspect to affiliate a person with the bourgeoisie only because of their conduct while ignoring their philosophical viewpoints. We can conclude that Arnold's tendency was, above all, to preserve his conventional roots rather than to support a revolution.

Eagleton's belief that Brecht, Rimbaud, and Picasso shared their rejection of the bourgeoisie is interesting in relation to Arnold. In this respect there is a difference. Arnold does not ignore bourgeoisie music in general, but extracts from it basic compositional elements, making use of them because of his own personal preference. He is attracted by development techniques used by the old masters, but also by Mahler and Sibelius; therefore, there is aesthetically no crime in using these elements. Presumably, Arnold was never really interested in whether he acted as a modernist, a traditionalist, an enfant terrible, or even a postmodernist. He is not interested, in this respect, in considering aesthetic concepts, and grants no direct relevance to such philosophical questions. If Eagleton investigated postmodernism because he was interested in the phenomenon itself, Arnold's investigation feels much closer to Chris Walton's postulation:

„...Von einer 'Postmoderne' in England zu reden ist jedoch widersprüchlich, wenn es dort keine eigentliche Moderne gegeben haben soll...will man die Bedeutung der Musik Englands in unserem Jahrhundert beurteilen, dann muss man die Werte der Moderne genauso hinter sich lassen, wie bei einer Beurteilung der Postmoderne, nämlich jene klischeehafte, historisierende Kategorie des ästhetisch Neuen und mit ihr den Glauben an das geschichtlich notwendige Verlassen der Tonalität...man muss bereit sein, eine empirische, stilistische und technische Vielfalt zu akzeptieren; und man darf nicht mehr vor einer Musik zurückscheuen, nur weil sie einfach schön ist..." (WALTON 1994:269).

"...To speak of 'Postmodernism' in England is nevertheless contradictory if there was no modernity there ...if one intends to judge the meaning of English music in our century, then one must leave the values of modernity behind, as in the case of a judgement about Postmodernism, namely the stereotyped, historic category of the aesthetically new combined with faith in the historically necessary abandonment of tonality...one must be ready to accept an empirical, stylistic, and technical variety; and one can no longer shy away from music just because it is nice..."

To treat Arnold as a postmodernist, however, would be contradictory, as would the idea of viewing him as a pure modernist. He refutes, by all means, aesthetic analysis and categorisation – and this may be why Arnold had to become an isolated phenomenon in English music for a time. In the sixties and seventies, when aesthetic discussions increasingly became the main agenda and "Adorno's Heirs" were expounding upon their rights, there were two possible reactions for Arnold: he could either change his style radically or try to position himself by simply writing music and hoping that his works would be categorised based on their own merit. He did this in his own peculiar way, often wearing himself down, which had an enormous impact on his psyche.

Arnold pursued his own idea of aesthetic reflection, which seemed at time to be almost missing entirely. It cannot be said that Arnold was "too stupid" to firmly position himself. From his point of view, and from the point of view of his compositional models Mahler and Sibelius, music had to speak for itself. If he intended to write a programmatic work, he would first create a suitable world of thoughts. "...Curiously, the first idea is usually a completely non-musical one; that is to say, it has nothing to do with notes. For example, what prompted me to compose *Beckus the Dandipratt* was the thought that the modern repertoire seemed to have nothing in the same category as *Der Freischütz*, that is, a work which...would have a sense of drama.[97] This came before any melodic, harmonic or dramatic ideas for the work itself..." (SCHAFER 1963:152-153).

If Arnold nevertheless wanted to compose a symphonic work belonging to the world of "accepted" music, he concentrated on the invention of material and used his entire vocabulary. It was a canon consisting of a wide range of possibilities and culminating in its most progressive form, as in Sibelius's symphonies. Arnold does not resist any of the influences of modern music. In contrast to other figures in contemporary British music, he applied a musical idiom using whatever he wanted to use. He did not think in categories like "serious" or "light". The fact that Arnold was not afraid to orchestrate John Lord's symphony for a rock band (Deep Purple) and a full symphony orchestra, and was not even afraid to fight for its success, reveals a lot about his openness to all fields of art.

Let us recall the three theses postulated by the author: 1. Arnold was compositionally influenced by more conservative poles (Sibelius, Mahler, and Berlioz) as well as by the second Viennese school; 2. Arnold felt free to choose the methods (compositional procedures, especially instrumentation) of his mysical style, staying well away from the concept of divided hemispheres of serious and light music; 3. Arnold's deliberately planned compositional polystylistic style made categorising him, in the old sense, almost impossible.

As a composer, Arnold is a unique and singular phenomenon. No case comparable to his exists. Indeed, there were always composers who apparently rejected tendencies towards progress, instead composing "as if nothing were happening".[98] These composers are now either a mere reflection of history and have been generally forgotten, or they are represented by a single work. Neither situation applies to Arnold, even if Cole, as already stated in chapter one, describes Arnold as a "victim...of partial representation" (COLE 1989:vii). Arnold is now omnipresent in British music, represented by such different works as *The River Kwai March, English Dances, Double Concerto for Two Violins and Orchestra,*

---

[97] The question of whether Arnold indeed created a work in the manner of Weber's *Freischütz* shall not be addressed.
[98] However, this conclusion is much too sharp and cannot applied to him.

126

the concert overture *Beckus the Dandipratt*, or his nine symphonies. His music has indeed gained a high level of acceptance, mainly in the Commonwealth countries; however, this is equally true of a large number of modern continental-European composers such as Wolfgang Rihm, Helmut Lachenmann, and Bernd Alois Zimmermann, whose works are rarely performed in Great Britain.[99] If Arnold's music is analysed in a manner that is free of aesthetic prejudices, its great compositional value can be seen and Arnold's position can be defined. But if one still thinks of Arnold in terms of current explanatory patterns (perception archetypes), the following, unfortunate often occurs: he is almost completely dismissed as a legitimate topic of musicological study. Hence Burton-Page's 1989 remark shall be used as a credo for any upcoming analysis of Arnold:

"...Those who confuse fertility with facility and do not see that the universal spirit also requires an individual voice for its expression. Malcolm, seeing – as a universal spirit must – that his art encompasses, but also goes far beyond, the pleasure principle, has in over half a century of music-making truly found his own individual voice. It is to his credit, and our enrichment, that it is audible in every bar of his mature music" (BURTON-PAGE 1989:165).

---

[99] This can be presumably led back to market mechanisms. *cf.* the current discussion led by Jörn Hiekel (HIEKEL 2006).

4. British Contemporary Music: Classical Thinking, Progress, Musical Life, the Market Economy, the General Public, and Aesthetic Categorisation within the British Modern Age: The Construction of Arnold's Image

5. *The Three Musketeers*: Too "Inauthentic" for a Real Reconstruction? Thoughts on the Compositional Material

It has unfortunately not been granted to Sir Malcolm Arnold to experience an audience's enthusiasm for his reconstructed ballet, *The Three Musketeers*. He was secluded in Attleborough, Norfolk, with his mobility greatly limited by illness and was unable to attend the production. He passed away on the day of the premiere, which took place in Bradford at the Alhambra Theatre on 23 September 2006.

However, "reconstruction" is actually an inexact term for the opus that was created and is now available to the general public. While the idea of writing a new ballet for the Theatre Royal, Covent Garden, harkens back to a creative meeting in 1975 between the composer and two British ballet choreographers and designers, David Drew and Terry Emery, the scenario sketched out at that time has not been realised, especially not in the production's current form.

Malcolm Arnold, known to the British public as an experienced, productive, and elegant creator of orchestral compositions, immediately fell in love with this project and enthusiastically sketched out drafts for this ballet[100] in the form of piano short scores.[101] The sketches consist of 13 fully completed short pieces of composition, usually limited in length to one page and named with programmatic titles taken from Alexandre Dumas's original novel. There is no further information available about how Arnold planned to elaborate on these sketches. From a superficial perspective, the pieces could be described as piano pieces of a moderate degree of difficulty, often evoking an impromptu character. Arnold's compositional approach can easily be seen by analysing the pieces' harmony, the development of their subjects, and their voicing structure (compositional layout/setting).

There may have been an economic as well as a technical explanation for why protagonists and promoters of the new stage version preferred to present a conglomerate, consisting of Arnold's famous orchestral works (with the exception of a single original composition entitled *Constance's Sad Dance)*, rather than using the original material to produce a reconstruction.

---

[100] Regarding the genesis of this project, *cf.* David Drew's statements in the programme book for the ballet production (NIXON 2006:7) as well as Anthony Meredith's comments (NIXON 2006:8). A detailed description of why the production was not realised in 1975 and how the misunderstanding between Malcolm Arnold and the management of the Theatre Royal, Covent Garden, occurred is found in Harris and Meredith's book (HARRIS/MEREDITH 2004:329-332).

[101] The sketches can be viewed by the public at the Sir Malcolm Arnold Manuscript Collection in the library of the Royal College of Music, London, registration "Miscellaneous MSS, No. 19".

Perhaps the reasons were less complicated. It is likely that they were not aware of generally unknown drafts of *The Three Musketeers,* in contrast to the sketches available in the Royal College of Music collection.[102] On the one hand, these drafts underscore that Malcolm Arnold did prepare sketches in a way that corresponded to the typical and more realistic image of a composer: a composer working on his musical ideas, polishing motifs, carefully considering his inventions, and, as a final step, arranging his first drafts by rewriting a piano short score for the later orchestration process.

On the other hand, in spite of their brevity the sketches reveal that Arnold's inventions would easily have provided a suitable basis for further elaboration. The first step of his procedure, creating piano short scores for ballet compositions, is not out of character and can be established by referring to the other autographic piano short scores of *Electra* and *Sweeney Todd.*[103] Arnold himself said he had used this procedure in the case of his earlier ballet, *Homage to the Queen.* In a letter addressed to David Webster, the general administrator of the Theatre Royal, Covent Garden, he points out:

"...Please forgive me for troubling you but I have been working on a ballet for the last eight weeks which is now complete and only remains to be orchestrated...As it will take all of my time for the next six weeks to orchestrate this ballet. I would be most grateful to receive a letter setting out the customary terms of agreement over a work like this..." (HARRIS/MEREDITH 2004:133).[104]

To return to the question of the ballet performance that actually too place: visitors to the premiere were confronted with an arrangement that fulfilled the "requirements of the market" rather than the fragmented but original musical text. The arrangement was put together in a suite-like form and was advertised as an original ballet by Arnold.[105] The latter point should at least be discussed with regard to aesthetic considerations; the author is of the opinion that this procedure is reminiscent of the traumas suffered by many contemporary composers of the twentieth and twenty-first centuries. It has been a common procedure that compositional

---

[102] The author was allowed to view these sketches while visiting Sir Malcolm Arnold and Anthony Day in Attleborough. Extracts from the sketches are supplied here for the general public. The manuscripts now belong to the Arnold Estate.

[103] Both piano short scores can be found in the Royal College of Music Manuscript Collection, registration number A, bound volumes, numbers 11 and 26.

[104] Harris/Meredith quoted from a letter found in the archives of the Royal Opera House, Covent Garden. Unfortunately, they missed the enormous importance of this rather short note regarding Malcolm Arnold's composition process.

[105] Even Anthony Meredith, co-author of the biography *Malcolm Arnold: Rogue Genius: The Life and Music of Britain's Most Misunderstood Composer* and therefore very well acquainted with the original genesis of the ballet, has no scruples and describes the process as follows: *"Arnold loves the dance world and wrote five ballets...The Three Musketeers, however, is his first full-length piece. The score, especially created for David Nixon's NBT production, comes from a wide range of his work, some of it written for films, the rest for the concert hall. It has been an organic process, almost having a life of its own..."* (NIXON 2006:8).

inventions, at first purely designed for the concert hall, were suddenly used in media exploitations (e.g., film soundtracks, advertising music).[106]

The argument in defense of the current production, that a large part of Arnold's symphonic works were narrative in nature and therefore using a composite score of famous works was preferable to using the original sketches of the intended ballet, does not stand up over time. To further argue that the short length of the sketches made them inappropriate for a proper reconstruction or revision in the form of a new orchestration by a competent composer is also questionable. The existing original piano short scores (particells) of Arnold's earlier ballets could have assisted a composer in drawing conclusions about how Arnold sketched basic thematic ideas for a ballet and how he later processed them into a full orchestral score.

Therefore, the author is of the opinion that the sketches for Arnold's ballet *The Three Musketeers* can be viewed as complete in a thematic and compositional sense. Therefore, nothing would have prevented a later elaboration by Arnold. No ostensible "inautheticy" or "poor quality" of the material prevented Arnold from writing this ballet or from beginning the actual orchestration process. In this case, Arnold simply decided not to start because no immediate market-demand, economic need or contractual necessity existed. He had not received a formal request; in fact, the project had in a way been thwarted by Arnold's own clumsy intervention. In addition, his health became increasingly worse during 1975 (HARRIS/MEREDITH 2004: 333 et seqq.).

In the following paragraphs, the author will introduce the first drafts (Ur sketch). Attention will be paid to information from what were, until now, considered "original" sketches. These sketches will be called, for simplicity's sake, the RCM (Royal College of Music) sketches. Well-chosen compositions will be examined in terms of form, motif motivical development, harmonics, and their *Gestalt*, and possibilities for further compositional development will be outlined.[107] By comparing the musical Ur-substance to another Arnold ballet, in this case *Homage to the Queen*, it shall be demonstrated that the thematic sketches of *The Three Musketeers* go entirely against prevailing opinion and perceptions of which normative formulae Arnold follows in both compositions. In conclusion, requirements for a possible reconstruction of the Ur setting will be described. However, whether or not a purely piano performance or a new orchestrated setting in keeping with Arnold's style should take place is a

---

[106] The example of Ligeti can be used in this context: the non-intended use of parts from *Atmosphères, Lux Aeterna*, and *Aventures* in Stanley Kubrick's *2001: A Space Odyssey*, vehemently negatively evaluated by Ligeti himself, cf. Troop in 1999 (TROOP 1999:138 et seqq.).

[107] The issue should be discussed in its academic sense, although the task would also attract the author himself. Before one can think of the realisation of such an issue, copyright clearance needs to be undertaken. However, some successful historical examples of reconstructed large symphonic works, for example Mahler's 10th Symphony completed by Deryck Cooke, could be a stimulus for the idea.

question of high aesthetic value but one that cannot be answered with any finality in this paper.

The Ur-sketch, in comparison to the RCM sketch, reveals a substantially briefer initial approach. Arnold often uses repeat signs (*Faulenzer, repeat slashes*), mostly in order to avoid having to write out harmonic ostinato patterns. A few scribbles and corrections can be found; however, they are very minimal, as Arnold tends to notate musical ideas in a very fluid way. Only when he is absolutely sure that he is pleased with an idea does he write it out. Except for a single piece in which scribbles and corrections can be found,[108] he composed 15 pieces named in the Ur sketch as follows: 1. *Milady* 2. *Buckingham* 3. *Musketeer's Dance* 4. *Porthos* 5. *Athos* 6. *Rochefort* (a melody fragment that will be separately discussed) 7. *D'Artagnan?*[109] 8. *Aramis* 9. *King* 10. *N.N., Moderato* 11. *Constance's Sad Dance* 12. *M. Bonacieux* 13. *One for All* 14. *D'Artagnan* 15. *Cardinal Richelieux* (also titled as *Cardinal, Buckingham, Pas de deux*).

Before we discuss individual musical phenomena, we shall focus on a formal comparison between the Ur sketch and the later, probably cleanly copied, RCM sketch. The sketches do not contain the same pieces; the Ur sketch consists of 15 pieces (16 if we count one crossed-out piece) and the RCM sketch of only 13.[110] Arnold has cleanly copied the following pieces from the Ur sketch, leaving them untouched: *One for All* (later entitled *Academy Theme*), *D'Artagnan, Aramis, Porthos, The King, M. Bonacieux, The Cardinal, Milady, Buckingham, Constance's Sad Dance,* and *Athos.*

The pieces in the RCM sketch that Arnold did not continue to work are therefore No. 3, the *Musketeer's Dance,* showing a complete waltz in ¾, mutating to a 2/4 in its middle section and later returning back to the original ¾; No. 6, the *Rochefort* melody fragment consisting of 12 bars and using alphabet-based notes on the chromatic rising scale[111] (beginning with the letter A, equated to middle C); No. 7, the *D'Artagnan?* piece that shown nothing in common with the later *D'Artagnan* in the RCM sketch; and three single-melody fragments formed out of the words "Milady", "Richelieu", and "De Winter". Interestingly, Arnold uses the "Milady" subject almost as a twelve-tone row for the melody voice of a

---

[108] He has rejected it completely; it does not appear in the RCM sketch.

[109] This "?" is Arnold's own notation. Because of the later appearance of another D'Artagnan piece (see No. 14), this piece should be regarded as a rejected piece in spite of its completeness.

[110] The counting of 13 pieces is taken from Harris/Meredith (HARRIS/MEREDITH 2004:330). Indeed, it is arguable in itself, because the D'Artagnan subject on the second score page of the RCM sketch was written down twice: as a single piece and as a combined contrapuntal setting combined with the *Academy Theme [One for All].*

[111] The same procedure has been applied by Arnold in his 7th Symphony, opus 113 (1973) as well as in his *Fantasy on a Theme of John Field for Piano and Orchestra, opus 116* (1975). Harris/Meredith and Jackson both refer to the strong personal dedication Arnold gave his children in his 7th Symphony: he uses the names of his children (Katherine, Robert, and Edward) in order to set them into "music" by the use of the letter notes alphabet (HARRIS/MEREDITH 2004:317-322; JACKSON 2003:154-162).

piece with the same title (an issue the author will focus on later); and finally No. 10, *N.N., Moderato.*

The fact that the *D'Artagnan* subject is later used as a counterpoint to the *One for All* subject is not evident from the Ur sketch, although a later handwritten note, "Musketeers 3 on [illegible]", could potentially be interpreted from that point of view. However, this is speculation.

In the RCM sketch, a short passacaglia-like piece is found on page 3, clearly composed as a saraband and referring in its musical style to the baroque, offering an almost pastiche impression. It is entitled *La Folia (18th century), Dance of Intrigue?,* and is not outlined in the Ur sketch. The fact that it should be of central meaning within the ballet can be established based on Drew's statements; he also points out that Arnold improvised this piece (HARRIS/MEREDITH 2004:331).

The Musketeer's Dance reveals a very clear physical image of an archetypal Malcolm Arnold piece; its clean typeface makes it easy to be transcribed and reconstructed. At the beginning of the ¾ waltz, Arnold confronts us with an easy diatonic melody, supporting *das Primat der Melodie (the primacy of melody)*[112] and creating a joyful and humorous impression with its dotted rhythms. At bar 6, Arnold adds a new component in the form of seventh chords accompanying the melody. At bar 14, he changes into a 2/4, creating the notion of a foxhunt or an English horse running through his use of a roguish melody in the lower voice combined with quiet, typical Arnold rhythms in the higher voice. In addition, the parallel motion of seventh chords is also a special stylistic means that Arnold uses in almost every one of his orchestral compositions.[113]

The reason that Malcolm Arnold did not include this piece in the RCM sketch is not at all evident and must relate to his personal preference. In terms of its form and structure, applying simple antecedent and consequent patterns, there is no difference between *The Musketeer's Dance* and other pieces in the RCM sketch.

---

[112] Ünlü has recently coined the very useful term „Primat der Melodie" *[primacy of melody]* in his study of Mahler's orchestration (ÜNLÜ 2007:22-25). The term is also very helpful and completely appropriate here. Arnold always emphasises the importance and audibility of solo voices through special instrumentation procedures. In this approach, he is very similar to Mahler – and it is also striking how much devotion he pays to Mahler in compositional aspects: "...In some works of Mahler one can find every kind of technical connection between statements by looking at the score, and yet in performance the unity and form of the music is often difficult to grasp. This slight obstacle which I have to surmount to enjoy some of Mahler's original and beautiful music is thus small as to detract from it as a whole. Since Mahler's death very few composers have used the wonderfully clear and clean sounds which he used to perfection..." (Arnold's statements in "I think in terms of sound", *Musicians* 1957, reprinted in Burton-Page's *Philharmonic Concerto*) (ARNOLD 1956:168).

[113] Apparently, Arnold does not think about hidden fifth and octave parallels. Maybe he even applies them on purpose...

Musketeer's Dance

Malcolm Arnold

Figure 30 Transcription, based on the Ur sketch[114]

Reproduced by kind permission of the Arnold Estate.

Arnold's idea for a thematic piece for the character of Rochefort
has remained only a fragment; nevertheless, he sketched out his inspiration
for a complete single melody composition in ¾, which is of enormous
informative value, giving us an understanding of his composition process.
He generated a tone row of the name R O C H E F O R T, using his
chromatic letter notes alphabet[115] (*cf.* illustration and the Rochefort tone
row, consisting of eight notes).

---

[114] Transcribed by the author.

[115] Nevertheless, Arnold's procedure cannot be called revolutionary – he did not invent the
letter notes alphabet, and there have been several famous attempts to convert the letters of the
alphabet into music, e.g., the famous B A C H motif, Shostakovitch's use of his own name, or
compositions by the Austrian composer and Hauer pupil Gerhard Rühm (born in 1930).
Nevertheless, it is interesting that Arnold, considering his demand "to write a good tune" as

Nevertheless, he has not become a slave to his own system. While generating the letters "R" and "O" from the letter notes alphabet, the next letters, "C" and "H", have been equated with the notes from the normative tone scale. He completely renounces the "E" (French language, muted "e"). The letters "F", "O", "R", and "T" are again generated from the letter notes alphabet. In order to musically round out the subject, which has so far been marked by its frequent tone repetitions, he complements new material, notating this a system lower than the Rochefort subject. This is not not based on the letter notes alphabet at all. Rather, Arnold complements the Rochefort melody with the still-missing notes from the chromatic scale, creating a counterpole between the two materials. The concurrent side effect becomes more visible. He stacks two different diatonic structures on top of each other: if the Rochefort melody is taken from the C-major Ionic scale, the second part represents the B-major scale starting on its second scale note (therefore, one could describe it as "B Dorian"). It becomes obvious that Arnold has pre-posed this contrasting effect within the subject material by using these two scales, narrowly crossed (by only a semitone) with each other. He has therefore predetermined a compositional status of high meaning from the very beginning.

essential, does generally apply such a deterministic procedure, found in his preceding works, opus 113 and 116! Although Jackson extensively and accurately analyses both works in relation to the letter notes alphabet (JACKSON 2003:154ff; 164 et seqq.), his conclusions seem a little far-fetched, as he wants to call Arnold a "serial composer": "At this stage in his career Arnold was seen as some sort of musical dinosaur...Magic squares and other process generators had long been used by both the serial and chance schools of composition and here Arnold shows that he, far from being isolationist, is fully aware of these tools..." (JACKSON 2003:161-162). The author believes that Jackson overemphasises the role of the letter notes alphabet, which Arnold only applies for material considerations. Arnold's basic application can probably be led back to his special situation in the seventies. A speculation: maybe he, struck by depression and manic-depressive attacks, needed a sort of tool to compose melodies. It is interesting that he completely stopped writing in 1978, having composed his 8th Symphony. He went back to composing in 1982 by writing the *Concerto for Trumpet and Orchestra, opus 125* (1982).

Figure 31 Page 4 of the Ur sketch, Rochefort subject

Reproduced by kind permission of the Arnold Estate.

In the piece *Milady*, the compositional material can also be traced back to the letter notes alphabet.[116] However, the system by no means overpowers Arnold. The first letter "M" corresponds to the expected note C, but already the letter "I" (which would have meant G sharp) is substituted with G, the latter more supportive of the tonality Arnold wishes to express. The next two notes, B and A, can be equated with the letter "L" (letter notes alphabet) and the letter "A" (onomatopoeic A=A); for the letter "D", he notates the two possibilities in his sketch: D (onomatopoeic) or D sharp (letter notes alphabet); the final tone, B flat, stands for "Y" (*cf.* illustration).

Now Arnold proceeds comparably to the Rochefort subject. He complements the material by using the full chromatic scale and composes, now in command of a twelve-tone row, a waltz in his own voice. Above all, the contrast between the melody voice and the accompanying chords is very interesting. He opposes the first five notes, virtually settled on white

---

[116] The material is found in the Ur sketch, page 6.

keys, with a highly chromatic and dissonant chord setting in the form of an ostinato, lasting two bars (bars 1-4). The moment the tonal material of the melody line strongly approaches the black keys, Arnold changes the tonal character of the accompanying chords. He then prefers substantially consonant sounds (for example, the C-minor seventh-ninth chord in bar 8).

Nevertheless, the switch between black and white keys – between upper and lower voice – occurs in an overlapping way; it does not start at the first initial black note, E flat, in bar 5. This may point back to bar 6: the two-bar ostinato has not yet been completed.

The idea that this black-and-white painting is a compositional coincidence seems doubtful. Although intuition might have played a role, Arnold always tends to create a balance between the diatonic and the chromatic. Arnold reveals his aesthetic view in his conversation with Murray Schafer in 1963. Acknowledging his preference for the diatonic system and seeing a danger of arbitrariness within the chromaticism of contemporary music, he tries to explain his own standpoint. Arnold's inclination to integrate both elements, the diatonic and the chromatic, into his own approach of writing tunes now seems explicable. To create a balance within the logic of the melody, it needs both elements:

"...A r n o l d: A melody must have both strength and weakness if it is to be expressive. To my ear, the diatonic system affords the best opportunity for creating melodic ideas that possess both these features to a maximum degree. The further a melody moves away from its tonic, the weaker it becomes, and the more it needs the tonic to complement this weakness. This is what I have against atonal music: it leads to a state of musical meandering. This is of course personal to my ear, and is in no way a criticism of anyone who writes that way..." (SCHAFER 1963:153).

The arrangement of the actual melody (cf. illustration) is reminiscent of the use of freedom of another "Arnold": Arnold Schönberg.[117] Indeed, an application of the twelve-tone technique (cf. illustration) cannot be further worked out because the subject itself immediately leads to a transitional episode in which Arnold focuses on the harmonic progression of chords. The fact that Arnold may possibly have used retrograde forms or other row variations, or even transpositions of the tone row, is rather unlikely – Schönberg's techniques are not found in Arnold's whole oeuvre.

---

[117] I.e., in spite of the twelve-tone row, single tones of the row may be repeated several times, or two successive tones can be used as quasi-trills or tremolos.

Figure 32 Page 9, excerpt from *Milady*, RCM sketch. (The numbering of the notes is added by the author.)

Reproduced by kind permission of the Arnold Estate.

Figure 33 *Milady* tone row, excerpt from the Ur sketch (see "M.")

Reproduced by kind permission of the Arnold Estate.

Let's examine more closely the question of the basic shortness of all Arnold's introduced thematic ideas.

The presented sketches can, in this respect, only be called principal theme overviews. Arnold does not outline any thematic structures or contrapuntal additions, but it is very likely that he would have added them in the final process of orchestration. By following a "mind game", this point can be underscored further: if one compares his ballet *Homage to the Queen*, composed in 1953 for the coronation of Queen Elizabeth II and consisting of similar short pieces with thematic as well as functional titles (*Earth, Water*, but also simply *Pas de deux*),[118] to the sketches for *The Three Musketeers*, Arnold's composition procedure becomes obvious. It is very easy to reduce the pieces from *Homage to the Queen* to their monothematic or dualistic main structures. If one uses this method, the fact that the sketches for *The Three Musketeers* seem pure or naïve no longer seems at all surprising.

But why shall we compare only these two pieces? There are several reasons. The quoted letter, already mentioned, shows that Arnold did write piano short scores. The fact that, in the case of *Homage to the Queen*,[119] the short scores no longer exist does not prohibit use of a methodical, comparative approach, but rather supports it. Further, the formal construction, the applied harmony, and the compositional core elements are, in many places, the same.

Both works have an introduction in which a fanfare-like melody is used, creating a majestic opening frame. While in *Homage to the Queen*

[118] However, Arnold's ballet *Electra*, composed in 1963 as a ballet in one act, shows a continuous structure. It is a full symphonic tone poem, without general separated single pieces.

[119] Two Arnold ballets, *Electra* and *Sweeney Todd*, were first composed as piano short scores; see the Royal College of Music Manuscript loan collection.

the long E-flat pedal note evokes vague associations with Mahler's 1st Symphony, in *The King* Arnold uses pedal triads in the form of a tonic upper-fifth octavo setting (from bar 1 on, B flat, from bar 3 on, C) very effectively as accentuations. Possible support by the full orchestra apparatus is also indicated by the descant voice (see illustration). It does not require a lot of imagination to see the possible bombastic orchestration Arnold could have easily applied to this.

The first eight bars (see transcription) are followed by a short transitional episode: interplay between the woodwinds and the brass. The woodwinds answer the brass section's fanfares in the same phraseology and in its reverse. From letter A on, Arnold shows off: other wind fanfares are supported by accented quick figurative runs in the strings – nevertheless, they serve no thematic function and lead only to the march, beginning in letter B and marked *marziale*.

Hommage to the Queen Prelude and Opening Scene

M. Arnold

Figure 34 Transcription of *Homage to the Queen*, initial fanfare (excerpt) and the marziale theme[120]

Homage to the Queen, op. 42
Music by Malcolm Arnold
© Copyright 1953 Paterson's Publication Limited.
All Rights Reserved. International Copyright Secured.
Reproduced by permission.

Both marches show very similar characteristics and both have a fundamental bass, moving in a stepwise motion in minims, later in pulsating crotchets when a two-bar sequence motif, based upon a simple descending major scale, follows. The single sequence steps are

---

[120] Piano transcription by the author.

chromatically descending in form, in bar 12 on F, in bar 14 on E, and in bar 16 on E flat. The subjects of both marches are based on diatonic triad notes of the respective beat harmony. Rhythmically, the *Homage to the Queen* march may be more inventive because of its extremely dotted notes in the beginning – later they appear in a quaver movement and even in a triplet movement at the end. However, in the *Homage to the Queen* march, one cannot find such an interesting syncopation effect as in *The King* march (*cf.* b. 18-19).

Arnold further tends, in *Homage to the Queen,* to combine harmonic chord progressions by the use of leading tones, e.g., the G-sharp-minor seventh chord will lead into a C seventh-ninth chord (leading tone procedure). In bar 5 and thereafter we can find the same procedure; he applies either a leading tone continuation or a chromatic modulation (the D-flat chord is approached by the preceding C-major chord with its added major seventh). In *The King* march, it is interesting to note how Arnold "dyes" the diatonic chord setting of the first part, sometimes enriched by seventh suspensions (bars 6-11), into a substantially more dissonant chord setting in the second part of the march. While the bass follows a sequence model (as already described), the melody and the rhythmic structure – consisting of mainly dotted notes in the first part of the march – is then developed by Arnold.

The dissonance relations, appearing in harmonic regard (*cf.* bar 15: the major seventh between A and G sharp; see also bar 19), do correspond well to the melody, which is more and more aggressively sharpened and focused by the use of semiquavers.

If we now look at the analysis of sections $\boxed{D}$ and $\boxed{E}$ of the *Homage to the Queen* march, the reason is simple. The counter-subject, appearing mainly in quaver triplets, can be compared in its function to the second part of the *King* march. The purpose of this analysis is to point out the common characteristics in the compositional annex of both ballets – consequently underscoring their compositional equivalence. It is therefore difficult to understand the reasons that almost no original material from *The Three Musketeers* was used in the current production.

Figure 35 *The King*, RCM sketch. (The structural elements are similar to the opening scenes from *Homage to the Queen*.)

Reproduced by kind permission of the Arnold Estate.

Although not all pieces of the various sketches can be discussed in depth within the scope of this study, we can identify a basic trend. Malcolm Arnold's original compositional material, composed in a highly creative moment full of passion, could definitely serve as a basis for further elaboration leading to a full ballet composition. In some places, he could have renounced the usual stereotypical patterns, for example in formal, rhythmic, or harmonic regards (*cf.* the much too frequent use of *da capo al coda/al segno*). Arnold did not work on details; however, this is not surprising, since he was working on *sketches*.

Considering the fact that similar sketch material – in particular concerning Arnold's use of the letter notes alphabet – is available and that Arnold, for instance, composed a full-length, three movement-long 7th Symphony by writing only five sketch pages, it is again even more incomprehensible that the protagonists of the *Three Musketeers* production did not think of a careful reconstruction of the original material.

The presented solution of creating a composite score of his most famous works suitable for the audience and taking up the original 1975 idea but neglecting the original material is rather reminiscent of the beginnings of the century of silent movies, in which pianists used to play from composition compendia like Ernö Rappée's[121] encyclopaedia, which consisted of suitable pieces for any emotional situation on screen – even sorted alphabetically. The author tends to believe that a real creative pianist completely renounced this collection and improvised, acting as a composer himself.

To return to Arnold: the conclusion is that the available sketch material should either be academically discussed or be used by experienced composers to reconstruct the meaning of the original ballet. Indeed, one would have to renounce another of Arnold's "full-length" works. As a result, with a reconstructed but fragmentary ballet, one would receive a true insight into Arnold's thoughts, hopes, and longings.

The Three Mustketeers, in its current, distorted form caters only to the perceived desires of the audience. Reconstruction or supplementation techniques may help us to trace Arnold's true intentions.

---

[121] *cf.* Prendergast's historical description of the practise of the silent movie era (PRENDERGAST 1992:6-18).

Figure 36 Malcolm Arnold (1948)

Reproduced by kind permission of Anthony Day.

Figure 37 The 1ˢᵗ Malcolm Arnold Festival 2006 in Northampton

Figure 38 (from left to right): Matthew Perkins, Günther Koegebehn, Cornelia Führbaum, the author, Gerhard van der Grinten Esq., Anthony Day.

Figure 39 Sir Malcolm and Anthony Day (2001)

Reproduced by kind permission of Anthony Day.

Figure 40 Sir Malcolm and the author (February 2006) in Attleborough

5. The Three Musketeers: Too "Inauthentic" for a Real Reconstruction? Thoughts on the Compositional Material

6. Maturity: Symphony No. 6

Arnold's Symphony No. 6 (opus 95) was completed in July 1967. It is a symphonic work arranged in three movements, scored for a full orchestra comprised of a woodwind section and complemented by the typical Arnold brass instrumentation of 4 horns, 3 trumpets, 2 trombones, 1 bass trombone and 1 tuba. Arnold uses the standard string section and a large percussion section that only really comes to bear in the second movement. The BBC Northern Symphony Orchestra in Sheffield first performed the work in June 1968 under the direction of the composer.

An important influence on Arnold in the first movement, *Energico,* is the improvisation of the American bebop saxophonist Charlie Parker, also known as "Bird"[122]. Notable characteristics of Parker's style include arpeggios of seventh chords and scales and in particular runs and licks to the tonic via chromatic 'leading' tones, often combined with passing tones.

These "bebop approach notes", [123] combined with linear arpeggios create particular passages around which the first movement is based. However, Jazz harmonies using the full cadence II-V-I are avoided.

Charlie Parker, Improvisation über "Confirmation" (C. Parker), 1946

Auszug 6. Symphonie, 1. Satz, T. 14f Flöten, Oboen und Klarinetten

Figure 41 Comparison of Parker/Arnold phrasing

Arnold's 6th Symphony begins with furious semiquaver arpeggios creating a two-bar harmonic field which drifts between A major/A minor and F[sharp] major/F sharpminor. Pizzicato is added to this almost motto-like woodwinds passage lending it a sharp percussiveness which accentuates the dynamic contrast between piano and forte. The most important element, however, is the uncertainty that originates from the presence of major and minor thirds and the immanent discord. The balance between

---

[122] This influence is apparent through musical analysis and is also referred to in Cole and Jackson's established works on Arnold. It can thus be assumed that both authors, through their close friendship with the composer, were convinced that this was the case, especially according to Cole's book published by Arnold's publisher Faber.
[123] Terminology used by Berklee College of Music, Boston (USA), cf. various teaching material.

major and minor later influences the linear development (see first subject), as well as the vertical harmonics (e.g. jarring seconds and sevenths in the brass chords). The contrast between C natural and C sharp is neither a typographical error nor mere 'colouring', but deliberate and clearly articulated writing.

Figure 42 Symphony No. 6, 1st movement, b. 1f, extract from orchestral score and piano reduction of harmonies

Symphony No. 6, opus 95, © by Faber Music Ltd. Reproduced by permission. All Rights Reserved.

This polyphonic two-instrument passage is followed by a 'heavy' passage in the third bar. The whole brass section plays a quaver-long *ff* chord with the notes A#, C#, F#, A, C and E. At the same time, the strings join in holding on to the chord at *piano* to create a notably resonant effect. The chord structure clearly refers back to the tones of the first two bars. While in the first chord the sevenths[124] A#-A and C#-C are arranged linearly, in the second chord it is the ninths G-A flat and D-E flat which dominate. These two harshly-accented chords (see piano extract bars 3-11) then regularly recur every four bars until the start of the subject (bar 28), interrupting Arnold's bass ostinato always on beat 3+.

---

[124] 'Diminished octaves'.

Figure 43 Symphony No. 6, 1ˢᵗ movement, bars 3-11, two-chord formations and the "resonance" in the upper strings in addition to the "nervous" original ostinato

The ostinato which appears for the first time in bars 3-11 is not only reminiscent of a jazz double-bass player in its instrumentation (Arnold scores pizzicato for celli and basses), but also evokes a nervous, almost stuttering effect through its hectic semiquaver motion. The ostinato phrases are arranged in the form of question and answer (4+4). The "answer" relates to the question in terms of rhythm and outline in which the pitch varies irregularly by either a semitone or a full tone (transposed). It is only because of this similarity between bars 4-7 and 8-11 that we can use the term "answer" here.

In terms of composition we have, up to this point, been exposed to three layers – the layer of tied chords or 'resonance' in the upper strings, the accented brass and the bass ostinato. To this Arnold adds another contrapuntal layer in the woodwinds from bar 12f. In the following eight bars (12-19) the *proper* bass ostinato appears which will continue to occur in this form for the rest of the first movement.[125] It is similar to the original ostinato in bars 4-11, yet it possesses a more ordered structure. It

---

[125] Arnold often presents the listener with a 'motto' before the proper 'statement'.

is formed from two-bar cells dominated by arpeggios, namely G major, A minor and F sharp major. The ostinato also contains two hidden lines of seconds that conclude with an interval of a third – rising seconds G-A flat-A (bars 12, 14, 16), falling seconds E flat-D-C sharp (bars 13, 15, 17). The rhythmic form is drawn across two bars and repeated three times. The outlines of both two-bar phrases move in a similar direction with the intervals differing slightly from each other (*cf.* the even and uneven bars of the ostinato). The type of harmony used until bars 13-14 is a broken triad in 2nd inversion.

Figure 44 Bass ostinato in bar 12ff

The woodwinds layer introduced from bar 12 then emulates Charlie Parker's improvisation, creating a contrasting counterpoint to the ostinato and the chord layers that were prevalent until that point. A detailed analysis allows us to draw conclusions about the following basic forms used by Arnold.

Figure 45 Basic forms – contrapuntal 'Parker' layer in b. 12-19

The ostinato repeats once (b. 20-27) before the entrance of the first subject in bar 28 (letter B). The first subject has an interesting internal structure. While four motifs can be identified (annotated with w, x, y and z in the figure) the question of syntax is less obvious. The diversity in w, x and y in bars 28-31 suggests a phrase structure of 3+3+2 and 3+2+3 (the extent to which bar 33 can be included therein is uncertain). The literal repetition of w transposed to C sharp in bar 32 would, however, support the assertion that this is a simple 4+4 structure. Due to the abruptness and "short-winded" nature of the motif this problem cannot be fully resolved. The only certainty is that a 2+2+2+2 division, like the bass ostinato, is impossible as x goes into y almost seamlessly (with overlapping 'phrases') with no logical two-beat division.

Elements   w: major/minor ambiguity
x: falling scales
y: Seconds and sevenths as changing
notes followed by a semiquaver
Repeated notes/'tremolando'
z: rising arpeggio of a seventh chord[126]

Figure 46 1st subject

Symphony No. 6, opus 95, © by Faber Music Ltd. Reproduced by permission.
All Rights Reserved.

The semiquaver movement in the violins up to bars 33-34 demonstrates Arnold's desire for a "motor effect" with the motif w picking up Parker's nervous "speech" from the beginning (in particular b. 6). Triads and seconds are the most important intervals. The complimentary interval of minor second/major seventh in y′ can be seen as a further development of y (which uses seconds).

The *ff* chord in bar 43 halfway through the third beat is followed by a short rewritten section (b. 44-55). Over the quavered "walking bass" in the celli and basses completing the fourth, w appears in various forms - w‴ in the strings and oboes is confined to the minor third (b. 47); bar 48 introduces horns, trumpets and piccolo, but here on the offbeat on beat 4,

---

[126] z also occurs briefly in bar 15.

almost as a delayed "echo". Finally b. 53ff trumpets, horns and piccolo are answered by the offbeat echo in the strings and oboe. Flutes, clarinets and bassoons are added to the two bass ostinato and the w layers prevalent so far, creating six voices in held whole note chords, which refer back to the chord structures in bars 3 and 7. A fourth element is introduced in bars 47ff and 53ff in the form of a single note swelling from piano to *ff* which finishes with a major third leap. This initially inconspicuous idea develops into one of the movement's defining elements in bars 135-154 where it is expanded increasingly in the composition (see examples below).

Posaunen, Tuba

Figure 47 "Inconspicuous idea" (bar 47f)

In clear contrast, the second subject follows, beginning at bar 56. At first it is 10 bars long with its syntactic structure manifesting itself in 6+4; its motion is characterised by long notes and a wide ambitus. To some extent there is a development of the motifs in the first subject. The first three bars have already appeared in similar form as w′′ (b. 33) and the rising semiquaver arpeggio is still similar to z.

The second subject is, however, in contrast to the first, devised without caesurae and is therefore more fluid; it emphasises lyrical components (for instance the 'pause' on F as seventh of the fundamental G [b. 60]) which means that, despite the close connection, one can point to contrasting thematic dualism.

The instrumentation is one factor that contributes to this effect. The second subject is scored in the bass and is initially performed in unison. The nervous seconds used as changing notes (y′), which we can recognise from the first subject, act as a counterpoint in the woodwinds and horns and are arranged as a chord layer. Arnold also cleverly changes the register in the woodwinds (cf. clarinet/oboe) to create a very different, much more "raw" sound.

Figure 48 2nd subject, first "appearance" (b. 56)

The second subject is repeated once, this time on G (b. 65, E) not A sharp and with a change in instrumentation. The unison section is played by the 1st and 2nd violins, viola, flute, oboe and clarinet with the seconds as changing tones appearing in the horns, bassoons and tuba. Looking back, we can see that at this point Arnold reveals the arrangement in thirds (A sharp= B flat and G) that he had planned from the beginning. The fact that the accented brass chords in the introduction vary between A sharp and G is an element in the construction which applies to the first movement as a whole. Instead of the usual tonic-dominant relationship, this is replaced with a mediant relationship.

The solid crotchet brass chords in bars 74/75, which occur at the same time as the nervous E-A-E semiquaver rhythms in the timpani, cause the harmonic functional analysis to break down, leaving only variants. The question is, what is the tonic fundamental? It could possibly be the tuba's E, which through the timpani's A degenerates to an undifferentiated "bassy pulp". The problem then is how to explain the following bass ostinato entry on G. But if one interprets the chords as only sounds without function, as might be suggested by jazz chord symbols, it is easier to understand the harmonic thinking. A polytonal A minor/F sharp minor chord with E in the bass leads to two interwoven diminished seventh chords – Em⁷ and Fm⁷ – disrupted by a barrage of perfect fifths A-E in the timpani. The predilection for seventh chords already witnessed in Arnold's *Sonata for Piano* appears again here in its purest form. In particular, Arnold prefers to obscure its harmonic effect by means of a bitonal configuration.

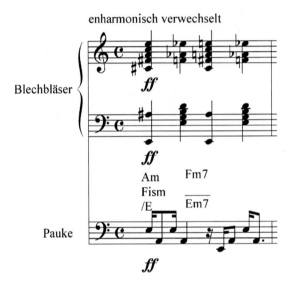

Figure 49 polytonal 'block', enharmonically spelled

Symphony No. 6, opus 95, © by Faber Music Ltd. Reproduced by permission. All Rights Reserved.

This 'polytonal block' takes on a more formal than harmonic function. It "behaves" like a two-bar piece of a puzzle that Arnold has "stuck in" his composition to ensure a quick and problem-free transition, in this case to the "development" starting at bar 76.

The term "development" should, however, be replaced by the term "reworking" because, as will be demonstrated, an analysis of the first movement based on the sonata form would be misleading.

Bars 76-91 bring a literal repetition of bar 12ff, where there are marginal differences in instrumentation – the flute voice is represented by a single piccolo and the harsh brass accents have disappeared. At least by letter $\boxed{H}$ (b. 101) the sonata form which Cole and Jackson elaborated becomes ad absurdum. Superimposed on the contrapuntal polytonal arpeggios in C-major/C -minor and A-major/A minor in the strings (reference to bars 1-2), Arnold develops a lyrical third subject with intervals reminiscent of Bartók or Walton.

Indeed the third subject bears a striking similarity in form and intervals to the fugue subject from Bartók's *Music for Strings, Percussion and Celesta.* If we set aside the different metre and rhythm, Arnold, like Bartók, makes several 'run-ups' before realising the subject in its entirety and bringing it to a dramatic height before concluding with a drawn-out version of the first motif.

Figure 50 3rd subject

The two elements which comprise the third subject are the "Bartók motif" on the one hand, which is composed of a rising minor second followed by a minor third leap with a falling second, and the run of falling seconds on the other. The long note values, combined with the slowing effect of the rising crotchet triplets (b. 107, 109, 111) which contrast with the continuous semiquaver movement in the chord layer (strings) allow the third subject to be viewed as an independent entity and not as "re-worked" material, thus earning the title "subject".

The presentation of the third subject in bars 101-117 is then joined by an overlapping repetition of the subject itself (b. 117-133), but now written for violins and counterpointed by brass and low strings (arpeggios). The extremely percussive effect of this "re-scoring" is contrasted by the octave displacement of the subject in the violins.

Figure 51 6th Symphony, 1st movement, b. 113-121

In bar 135 (letter K) the "inconspicuous idea" described in bar 47 finds its compositional form. Added to the walking bass line in the celli and basses (*ref.* b. 46, using interval of a fourth) and the trill-embellished accented chords (*cf.* the introduction) is the extended crescendoing note that occurs three times (D, G#, E). In contrast to bar 46, this time the crescendo concludes with two energetic *ff* semiquavers in second interval. At the climax in bar 152, these semiquaver leaps occur four times in an almost manic ascension until the transition in bar 154 puts an end to the mania and reverts to the "recapitulation" at bar 156ff.

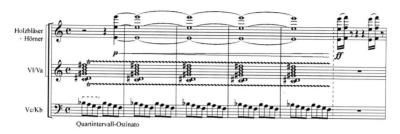

Figure 52 6ᵗʰ Symphony, 1ˢᵗ movement, b. 147ff

This "recapitulation" (b. 156-171), which now sees the subject re-scored for unison strings and horns, adds a new two-bar ostinato, this time in harmonic form. Arnold here again picks up one of the chords from the harmonic "block" – an F sharp major triad with the root in the fifth building on the A.

The second chord comprising B-E-B-G sharp-C sharp-E sharp only hints at the E-E sharp dissonance within the chord. Even if this is re-interpreted as an enharmonic D flat major chord with a C flat in the bass, the role of the E (or F flat) may be unclear. The repeated C triplets in the woodwinds and horns (from b. 186ff) now start on G from bar 203. The fact that Arnold gives this ostinato so much room – this huge crescendo to the start of the third subject lasts an astounding 34 bars – can only be explained by the tense seconds and sevenths. The dissonance of the layer of repeated notes clashing with the chord layer (C-C sharp and G-G sharp) is ultimately employed to increase tension. The actual overall orchestral effect of the two restricted layers (the chord ostinato and note repetition) is huge and reminds the listener of Holst's symphonic tone poem *The Planets.*

Figure 53 6th Symphony, 1st movement, b. 204-207 chord ostinato combined with note repetition and dissonant effects of C-C sharp and G-G[#]

Symphony No. 6, opus 95, © by Faber Music Ltd. Reproduced by permission. All Rights Reserved.

Those expecting the crescendo to climax in the first subject will be disappointed by the entry of the third subject (b. 209-225). This begs the question: which of the three subjects is the main subject and whether Arnold is thinking in terms of the traditional subject arrangements in sonata form at all. A pure statistical analysis of this question shows a dominance of the third subject.

The first movement ends humorously, almost with a wink from the composer. In bars 226ff he confronts us with the "original" bass ostinato of bars 4-7. The first two bars of the movement are repeated in bar 234, but without the percussive string pizzicato, closing in bar 236 with a quaver on a low A.

Overview of 1st movement form

Bars	Form
1-27	Introduction
28-43	1st subject
44-55	Transition to 2nd subject
56-74	2nd subject, presented in two 10-bar variations
74-75	'Broken' transition, harmonic block
76-101 (beat 1)	'Development', start of re-worked section, begins at b. 76 and closely corresponds to letter A, instrumentation slightly modified
101-116/117	3rd subject in the oboe (16-bar)
117-133/134	Repetition of the 3rd subject in the strings, arpeggios in the woodwinds and lower strings
135-154	3x *pp cresc. ff*, colour changed with trills, reference to b. 47ff
156-171	Recapitulation of the 1st subject
172-173	Identical to b. 74-75
174-208	Harmonic ostinato coupled with triplets on the same tone
209-225	3rd subject
226-end	Coda, start is same as bar 1

Figure 54 6ᵗʰ Symphony, 2ⁿᵈ movement, introduction and 1ˢᵗ subject (b. 7-22)

The second movement, *Lento-allegretto-lento*, opens with a unison *ff* 'B' in the woodwinds, with the first beat marked precisely by a pizzicato 'B' in the 1ˢᵗ and 2ⁿᵈ violins. The movement thins out section by section, with the oboes dying away first followed by the clarinets, until the flute/piccolo's transitional 'B' is relieved by a four-bar *pp* chord layer in the strings in bars 3-6.[127] The "switching" between major and minor, which Arnold consistently uses in the 1st movement, continues here as he subtly yet affectively obtains dissonance from the seconds in the chord. While the full B flat major sound in the lower strings (b. 3) is alienated by a high B natural in the 2nd violins, the polytonal G major is juxtaposed to B flat major in bar 4 (B-B flat dissonance). The same applies to the following bars - C sharp minor juxtaposed against A minor (b. 5, $C^{\#}$-C) and A minor, at least with the third C in the bass, juxtaposed against C sharp minor (b. 6, $C^{\#}$, C).

These four "basic" chords of the 2nd movement form the harmonic accompaniment layer for the 1st subject (A) which begins in unison in bar 7 with the oboes, trumpets and 1st violas. It is 16 bars long and syntactically divided into four-bar phrases, i.e. A-A'-B-C. A is written in the order $D^{\#}$-E-$C^{\#}$-C-F and the tones are repeated in that order until the 4th note, where Arnold adds the notes $F^{\#}$, G sharp and A. Motif A has a simple rhythmic form. A crotchet rest is followed by a crotchet movement that is stopped by two minims. Arnold only employs crotchets in the repetition/extension of the succession. A is now transposed down a semitone and becomes the sequence A′ in bars 11-14. Arnold also "bends" the interval structure by changing the minor third from note 2 to 3 into a major third. The same technique is applied in the next bar where perfect fifths (b. 8) become perfect fourths. It is not a true intervalled sequence as Arnold only maintains its shape.

Phrase B comprises two – two rising semitones answered by six crotchet triplets – in the chromatic movement and triad melody, with alternating thirds and sixths. C plays with the note $D^{\#}$ and after a diminished fifth C-F sharp the melody returns to the $D^{\#}$, this time with variations encompassing a greater range up to $F^{\#2}$. The 1st subject ends on a B with the note rising from below ($G^{\#}$-$A^{\#}$-B^{b}, b. 22) and "neutralising" the numerous chromatic swirls; this links back to bar 1.

There are three items in the 1st subject that are particularly striking.

The subject has a very restricted range (F^{1}-E) and dangles precariously from the central note $D^{\#2}$, avoiding extreme highs and lows.

Arnold again uses the structure of harmonic layer and melodic layer familiar from the 1st movement, which comes across in this context as less artificial.

The subject is composed of 2-bar units (arranged in 4+4+4+4) that are almost schematically modified. What help the subject come through is not the melodic or "genial" syntactic idea, but its scoring. The unusual unison mix of *pp* oboes, *pp* trumpets and *pp* violas, together with the various divisi muted strings and low clarinets, creates a tense, sombre atmosphere.

The author will group bars 23-39 together into A′ as Arnold returns to familiar stylistic material. The 1st subject appears in the low

---

[127] Here the clarinet, playing in its low register, adds either the third or the fundamental to the chord and is not truly used as a clarinet in terms of scoring or sound.

register of the celli and basses and is repeated until bar 38 with the held *pp* chords figured in the woodwinds. What is new about this section is the canon-like imitation of the subject an octave higher by the violas (tremolo, sul pont) and muted horns a bar apart. Indeed, Arnold makes small technical modifications to the chord layer (cf. bar 9 and bar 25 where the bass note disappears), but the schematically developed imitation with no contrapuntal additions gives further rise to suspicions of schematism, in other words, "the compositional abuse of time" within a space of 68 seconds.

    In bars 40-63 (B̄) Arnold extends the initial idea from the beginning of the 2nd movement with unison *ff* tones and unison octaves with added decrescendos appearing variously in the strings, brass and woodwinds, and then combines the idea into thematic three-note groups. In bar 40, B flat appears in the trumpets and high up in the strings and is answered by plucked strings enhanced by the brass only to be "startled" in beat 4 with the high, shrill D-octave in the woodwinds (piccolo, flute, oboes and clarinets). This results in the three-note group B flat-B-D. The "echo" in the 1st and 2nd violins (b. 43, D̄) is followed by three consecutive characteristic elements:

    the military-style entry on snare, bass and tenor drums combined with a cresc./dim. horn motif (non-transposed A, B in bars 44-46)

    the ostinato timpani fourths B flat-F

    the ascending scale movement in the celli/basses which already mark the transition from A′ to B (b. 39).

    The same process – a three-note group played by various sections and the three characteristic elements – appears again in bar 48 in the three-note group C-C$^{\#}$-E, in which the scale movement in the celli/basses is replaced by an alternating semitone movement in the horns at b. 55ff. This note group is found again from bar 60 on, with different dynamics. The intensity increases from *pp* to *ff*; and the percussion section also crescendos creating a logical transition to A″.

    A″ (b. 65-74) consists of two technical elements: the chord layer in the strings, which picks up the basic chords from A, and the solo trumpet which plays a mutated form of the 1st subject. Bars 64-67 actually refer to one rapidly diminuendoing form of the subject (cf. bars 7-14) with a note-for-note repetition from bar 68.

Figure 55 2nd movement, ostinato cells b. 75ff and b. 95ff

In $\boxed{C}$ (b. 75-102), Arnold initially confronts us with a new time signature (9/8) and a faster allegretto tempo. The style represented is very close to that of jazz and one method by which this is achieved is by the instrumentation. Pizzicato celli and basses pluck a two-bar ostinato, reminiscent of walking bass lines; parallel jazz seventh chords (typical for Arnold) are injected by punchy brass on a bed of percussion, which emphasises the offbeat character through the rimshots on every fourth quaver. The other method is by the bebop lines introduced in the flutes, oboe and clarinets from bar 86 that hint at the Charlie Parker style of the first movement.

Both elements show little variation; bars 77-94 are based on a single ostinato; from bar 95 there is a small variation in the intervals for the celli pizzicato and the brass harmonies (cf. figure 23). Even the tones used in woodwinds's bebop lines are confined to a very limited selection. The notes E, F$^{\#}$, G$^{\#}$, B and C sharp are selected in bars 86-94, and are used to create the E^{6} chord prevalent in popular music. Arnold makes use of the notes D, E^{b}, F$^{\#}$, A and B flat from bar 95 to form two chords - D major and E flat minor (F sharp changes to the enharmonic G flat). Although the shape of the bebop lines is similar and at least suggests a transposition of the first motif in bar 96, the interval structure is different, or to an extent "twisted", in notable places.[128]

---

[128] For a more comprehensive analysis of Jazz Chord Scale Theory, which is primarily advocated by Berklee College of Music, the author recommends Berklee publications and the following German-language publications: Jungbluth, Axel. *Jazz-Harmonielehre.*

Figure 56 2nd movement, bebop lines, b. 86ff

Symphony No. 6, opus 95, © by Faber Music Ltd. Reproduced by permission.
All Rights Reserved.

The following D section (b. 103-126/127) has less interesting motifs. Up to this point in the 2nd movement all the individual elements demonstrate either thematic ideas (first subject) or references to previous elements (bebop line approach in the 1st movement); in bars 103ff we now see endless ascending and descending scales scored in octaves within each orchestral section. D major up, A flat major down, A flat major up, D major down, D major up, A major down, E^b major up, a fragment of G major down, G major up, B flat major starting on C (or a mixolydian scale of C in jazz terms), F major; this continues until bar 118 where a low B major brass chord, enriched by horns and bassoons, breaks the pattern. Six bars of scales follow in a similar manner until the dramatic climax of the 9/8 section begins in bars 126/127, which the author has defined as section E (b. 126/127-138).

E is the most prominent example of the three-layer model. The now forte percussion is supported by heavy *f* brass throwing in recognisable C chords while the strings, unison in their *f* octaves, carry a new semiquaver motif. And even in this final element the brass harmonies and the new semiquaver motif deserve a more detailed analysis. Arnold

Funktionsharmonik und Modalität. Mainz: 1981 and Haunschild, Frank. *Die neue Harmonielehre. Volume II.* Brühl:1992

connects the polytonal chords to an ascending bass line in the bassoons and tuba (b. 127ff, G-G$^{\#}$-A-A$^{\#}$-B-C).

This line is reproduced in the first few notes of the new motif (at least until the A$^{\#}$, cf. figure 25), which has a sequential structure. Starting at bar 134ff, this structure culminates in C minor and C sharp arpeggios; the timpani roll on F interferes with the real bass note of C (tuba). Bar 139 invites tension; while horns, lower brass, bassoons and strings mark the C, high trumpets blare out an E major chord. This polytonal C major/E major configuration is again disturbed, this time more noticeably, by the timpani playing a D.

Figure 57 Structure of the musical climax in $\boxed{\text{E}}$

Symphony No. 6, opus 95, © by Faber Music Ltd. Reproduced by permission. All Rights Reserved.

Previous material is reused at this point, though in extended form (B′ 139-175). Arnold manages to pick out various motif fragments from individual sections of the movement and combine them in interesting mini variations. In this way, bars 139-144 correspond to bars 47-53, but with the pizzicato crotchets C, C sharp and E in the upper strings and also the brass fortissimo octaves shifted a crotchet forward. Arnold inserts seven bars of unison brass E-E^{b} (b. 146-152), accompanied by the familiar timpani B^{b}-F ostinato and drums before returning in bar 153ff to the horn motif of bar 55, scored for unison low flutes and bassoons.

Another repetition of A′ is seen beginning at bar 157. Due to the large-scale re-scoring this section (b.157-173), it has been identified as A′′′. The difference in sound is considerable, but is unaltered (e.g. in terms of counterpoint) with the exception of the added timpani ostinato.

Has Arnold simply re-scored this, more or less blindly copying what came before it?

Harmonic layer	Thematic layer	Canon imitation from b. 158
Piccolo, flutes, oboes, clarinets, trumpets, trombones, tuba, double bass	1st and 2nd violins con sord, violas con sord	Clarinets, bassoons, horns, va senza sord

The second movement finishes as it began, on an octave B swelling from *pp* to *ff*. Arnold allows the instruments to overlap in order to create a graduated blending of colours.

In conclusion, the second movement can be formally analysed as follows[129]:

Overview of 2nd movement form

Bars	Form
1-6	Introduction
7-22	A
23-39	A′
40-63	B
65-74	A″
75-102	C
103-126/127	D
126/127-138	E
139-175	B′
157-173-	A‴
174ff	Coda

The third movement, *Con fuoco* (crotchet = 144) is described in commentaries, in particular by Cole, as a "freely constructed rondo" of A_1-B-A_2-C-A_3-D-A_4 (COLE 1989:173). Indeed, at a superficial level this is correct, as the main subject (in varying lengths) always joins the episodes. Cole's divisions in his analysis ignore, however, that Arnold orders different musical ideas one after the other within the episodes that, due to their diversity, cannot in themselves be interpreted as a particular section. The author suggests the following in order to elaborate on Cole's analysis of form:

A_1 (b. 1-50), B (b. 51-107), A_2 (b. 108-122), C_1 (b.123-143), C_2 (b.144-180), A_3 (b.181-195), D (b.196-227), A_4 (b.228ff)

---

[129] One possible interpretation is a symmetrical ABA arrangement in which B would correspond to the 9/8 section (b. 75). This subdivision of the movement would, in the author's opinion, be too crude, as it does not allow sufficient room for Arnold's partly schematic repetition which is at the crux of the analysis.

Figure 58 6th Symphony, 3rd movement, rondo subject A₁

In contrast to the subjects in the first movement, the rondo subject in the third movement has a compositionally simpler structure. Formal repetition tends to dominate; the A major broken triad occurs five times in total. The unison melody is accompanied by two rhythmic string entries that have the characteristic of Rossini's *William Tell Overture*. The continuous repeated Gs, which are established over three bars at the end of the subject, balance out the A major tonality and make the listener expect a secondary dominant change to D major. Yet Arnold surprises us with a compositional trick. The succession G flat-F-E flat-D flat not only ends the subject, but the final D flat, too, becomes the new tonic fundament and from bar 18 onwards one sees a repetition of the entire rondo subject in the woodwinds and horns transposed into D flat major. Arnold also makes use of this technique in bar 32ff by modulating to F major via B, A, G and F, followed by another subject idea in the trombones. It could be argued that Arnold is in danger of "wearing out" the simply constructed subject by bending it so that by transposing it up and down a major third becomes natural and logical. The new "harmonic frame of reference" and altered instrumentation would appear to be the old one "reclothed".

In B (b. 51-107) Arnold again demonstrates his love of bitonal tension. In the strings, there is a contrast between instruments playing scales and those playing arpeggio chords (also later opposed to arpeggio chords) which is combined in various ways but predominantly in thirds (b. 51 G major/B major, b. 53 E flat major/G major, b. 69 C major/A flat major). This continuous polytonal section is interrupted only by an episode played in unison by the entire string section. The episode appears twice, and although it is written in 3/4, on closer inspection it contains a 5/4 beat

(b. 57ff and b. 83, now scored *ff* and intensified by the addition of the bassoons).

Figure 59 5/4 string motif

After the rondo subject is reiterated in diminuted A major form (A_2), Arnold picks up a motif in the lower strings (b. 90) and extends this into a soloistic element in the following C_1 episode. With a chord layer as a backdrop, characterised in the first movement by the equal presence of two neighbouring notes (e.g. bar 123, E flat/D and A flat/G), the aforementioned motif is quoted in a slightly altered form, arising first in the horns (b, 124f) then in the trombones (b. 127f), trumpets (b. 132f) and the woodwinds (b. 138f). The connection that Cole proposes between this motif and the beginning of the first subject from the 1st movement is, from a rhythmical perspective, marginal.

Figure 60 6th Symphony, 3rd movement, horn motif

The new section C_2, starting at bar 144, marks a change in style. Consecutive thirds build on the fundamental G, creating a chord which is accompanied by an extremely high, "hysterical" repeated triplet figure on C sharp played by the piccolo. This triplet loop begins with G minor scales. However, it is only when we recognise the E major and B major chord within the accumulating thirds that Arnold's compositional construction becomes clear. Similarly, the rondo subject in A major uses the major third connection to D^b major and F major as **consecutive** (i.e. linear) steps while at the same time Arnold arranges bitonal polarities vertically. The interference that the piccolo motif causes due to its high pitch is emphasised by the dissonance in relation to the C note in the chord.[130]

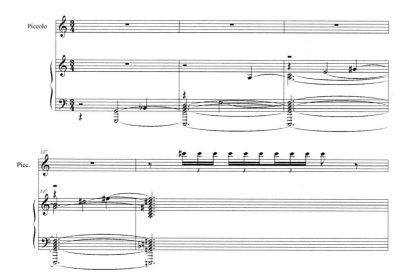

Figure 61 6th Symphony, 3rd movement, b. 144ff, bitonal polarity layered vertically

Symphony No. 6, opus 95, © by Faber Music Ltd. Reproduced by permission. All Rights Reserved.

This process repeats itself once (b. 155-164). The horn motif from bar 90 is picked up again in bars 165-176, and bars 177-180 act as a transition to the rondo subject at bar 181.

The rondo subject A_3 starting at bar 181, is scored exclusively for percussion and bassoon and has an ironic and minimalistic feel that is typical of Arnold's style. It shows his humorous side, which can also be seen in more popular works such as *A Grand, Grand Festival Overture* or *Beckus the Dandipratt.* Both, the instrumentation and style bear a striking resemblance to Britten's percussion variation on a theme by Purcell from his *Young Person's Guide to the Orchestra.* Whether Arnold was taking a page out of Britten's score in terms of the unexpected instrumentation he used (something he was not inclined to comment on) is possible, but is only speculation.

---

[130] It is also observed that the notes B^b and B (chord) as well as C and C sharp cause a dissonant effect.

Figure 62 6th Symphony, 3rd movement, A₃

Figure 63 Young Person's Guide to the Orchestra, percussion variation M

Episode D begins with an eight-bar chord ostinato in the brass (b. 196-203) to which pizzicato bass notes are added, played by celli and basses. The ostinato is repeated twice before a lyrical and somewhat more

172

serious subject (through its chromatic changing notes) begins in bar 204. While Arnold's pick-up of the ostinato technique is very similar to that in the 1st movement, this time the harmonies (around bar 204 where the string F major is set up against B flat minor) are realised in a new way. One could almost believe that Arnold disregarded his polytonalities, which are otherwise very calculated and grounded in related thirds, and composed the two layers completely separately, only later putting them together.

Figure 64 6th Symphony, 3rd movement, b. 204ff, "unintentionally polytonal?"

The 3rd movement closes with the rondo subject idea (A_4) in A major (b. 228ff), D flat major (b. 245ff) and F major (b. 262ff), followed by an almost endless Rossini-style galloping rhythm (b. 279ff) of D major and A major chords and a tubular bell, A major arpeggios beginning at bar 291, and an effective selection of instruments which, instrumentally, create a specific effect and serve to highlight the jubilant mood of the finale.

In conclusion, Arnold's 6th Symphony displays a definite reference towards very varied by repeated sections coupled with little variation in the subjects' motifs. The preference for clear models in terms of form stands out, whether it be the ostinato or rondo model or the literal repeats where only the scoring is altered. The danger of lapsing into simple repetition is something that Arnold counters in the first movement with the power of re-scoring, and even more so with the aforementioned close motif/subject relationship. The fact that the z motif of the first subject in the 1st movement occurs long before the first thematic idea and is reused in a different context as a notable polytonal stylistic technique emphasises the well thought-out structure, the "intellectualism" of the work. The references described in the analysis underline the strength of Arnold's desire to realise his "unity in form" idea.

Regrettably, the connections between the motifs in the second movement appear not to be conceived or developed in the same manner as those in the first movement. Repetition and ostinato are all too often mere "shells". The frequency of the repetitions, which at that point vary only in their instrumentation, gives the impression of a movement which has been "pasted together". The monotone rhythmic and melodic repetition in the 1st subject of the second movement is particularly noteworthy. Its monotonality and two-bar phrase structure inhibit any real possibilities for development.

By far the most important element of the 6th Symphony (also present in parts of his other works) is Arnold's polytonality. Arnold replaces the dominant-tonic relationship with that of thirds, this time not to colourfully seek new effects, as in his early work, but as a result of careful planning. By comparing the polytonality in the 6th Symphony with his early work, we can see a composer who is clearly more mature. The polytonal chords do not come, as for example was often the case in the *Sonata for Piano*, out of nowhere, but rather are logically prepared and meticulously developed.

The 6th Symphony can be described as having a four part construction. Unison voices take turns with harmonic passages, but for the most part the symphony is devised in layers. In general, Arnold composes in traditional layers such as the chord layer, thematic/melodic layer and contrapuntal layer. These layers are clearly recognisable in the construction and are also separated from the instrumentation.

7. *Symphony No. 9*: Reduction and Compositional Stringency

In this study, but also in current comments on Arnold's work, his tendency towards compositional reduction in his later works has often been discussed. Indeed, if one compares his early orchestral works with his later works, one can, at first glance, agree with this interpretation.

The overall understanding of the later works of every composer is accompanied by the concept that compositional maturity – even if acquired early – appears with age, and that it will eventually be reversed. Then, it is frequently stated, a composer becomes "childish", loses his skills, or goes mad.

Malcolm Arnold's 9th Symphony had to endure many of these judgements; even Charles Grove, a long-standing friend and supporter of Arnold's music, failed at first to persuade various orchestral managers of the fascinating strengths of the work: "...[Grove's widow reports] Charles had that score and he studied it and studied it...and he begged various people to do it...but no-one would touch it...people seemed to think that poor Malcolm had just gone round the bend and couldn't write music anymore and the 9th was just nonsense..." (JACKSON 2003:192).

Indeed, it is a credit to Jackson that he, among the present authors, has revised this view. In his detailed analysis of all of the symphony's movements, he follows a chronological path of analysis, picking out single phenomena and interpreting them from an analytical perspective. He even elucidates his position in an aesthetic regard (JACKSON 2003:192-197). We must therefore strive to understand Jackson's approach, and try to confirm it and critically supplement it.

The typical opening constellation of Arnold's orchestral works, in which he prefers a clear layer model (melody layer, counterpoint, and accompanying layer, mostly of a harmonic nature) is, in this case, rejected from the very beginning. The 9th Symphony (first movement in ¾, a vivace) opens directly with the subject. The subject is always stated in a two-to-three-part texture. The opening D-major triad is later imitated twice as a canon. While in the descant voice, mainly triadic arpeggios are applied (D major, B flat major, E flat major, A minor, F major), it is noteworthy that the upper voice is dominated by movements of seconds. Arnold does not shrink any interval combinations; he often directly approaches top notes using major sevenths (bar 13 or 15, letter A) or ninths (bar 16), revealing a notion of deep expression – despite, or perhaps because of, its two-part texture.

Jackson does not thematise the phrasing of the subject. In his published illustrations (most of them his own transcriptions), he has not even included all of the legato slurs. This could have inspired a noteworthy discussion, since Arnold follows an interesting procedure with regard to his phrasing. Indeed, the phrasing is mainly dominated by one-bar legato slurs; therefore, the triads within the subject are phrased in this manner in

175

the beginning. However, in bar 10, his illustration, which does not indicate every single legato slur (JACKSON 2003:193), suggests that the arppegiated E-flat-major triad should have been phrased in the same way as it had in the beginning. This is not the case; Arnold stresses the fifth-octavo leap instead.[131] In the full score, this is only a marginal procedural question, but the overall impact, in particular with regard to the actual performance of the work, is a definitively different question.

The initial scanty structure is maintained throughout the entire movement; however, the keyword is "structure". The structure of the subject is simultaneously amusing and distressing. The fact that it can be traced back to a clear definition of periodicity, divided into groups of 4 or 16 bars, is not of such great interest; however, in its musical striving, it almost creates the impression of a Perpetuum Mobile. Arnold tries to avoid a direct cadential effect; instead, he substitutes contrapuntal voices that correspond to each other in their rhythmic and expressive natures. It is probably the most extensive opening of any symphony by Arnold.

Jackson's evaluation is that "...It does not really settle anywhere. All the way through it is constantly on the move, never alighting in one key long enough for it to be thought of as home...." (JACKSON 2003:192-193). One can support this assessment, the resulting putative distracted state of the listener cannot be denied. Apparently, though, this distracted state is exactly what Arnold intended to achieve. By neglecting to bring closure to the music – also indicated by Arnold's original autograph, in which he did not use any scratchings or corrections at all (cf. original autograph) – the listener is left with a feeling of "...claustrophobia and entrapment" (JACKSON 2003:193). This is indeed a well-selected metaphor.

---

[131] The same can also be observed later: cf. A-minor and F-major triads that are taken on one single long bow (one slur).

Figure 65 *Symphony No. 9, opus 128*, 1ˢᵗ **movement, before letter** A

Jackson's statements concerning the major-minor ambiguity of the subject, ("...The melody keeps us guessing. Is it in D major or D minor?

Should it be an F sharp or an F natural, or is it moving to B flat?..." JACKSON 2003:192), however, must be qualified in this respect, as the subject can be interpreted differently. Arnold did not write a work in D major, but the subject itself addresses, aside from the tonic region, several regions of tonality that are borrowed from the tonality of D, regardless of whether they are major or minor. Thus the E-flat-major triad can be interpreted as a borrowed Neapolitan chord from the minor tonic, and F Major, A minor, and B flat major can be analysed without difficulty by means of the functional theory belonging to D major. Arnold's enharmonic spelling is unequivocal and agrees with traditional patterns.

It is also a pity that Jackson, who assumes Arnold used a subject structure of 16 bars, does not devote himself to the outlined three-part texture from letter $\boxed{A}$ on, classifying it instead as insignificant transitional material.[132] It is marked by high-level compositional skills, illustrating exactly the harmonic ambiguity that Jackson has previously stressed.

---

[132] Jackson describes the duets correctly; nevertheless, they already start at letter $\boxed{B}$ (JACKSON 2003:193).

Symphony No.9, opus 128, 1st movement

Malcolm Arnold

Figure 66 *Symphony No. 9, opus 128*, 1st movement, transcription[133]

If we look at Arnold's harmonic progressions from letter A on, it becomes evident that Arnold makes excellent use of chord suspensions, creating a harmonic tension and *détente*. The joining third voice is important because it makes these procedures possible. Arnold never aims directly for a harmony or a chord progression, but rather "laps" around them by means of suspension. In bars 19 and 20, the A major chord with the added major seventh (G sharp) is alienated in the lower voice by a fourth suspension on beat (D), first being resolved "correctly", but then leaping to B natural and moving step-wise into C sharp. In the following two bars, Arnold underscores his ability to spice up the harmony. Even if one fails to interpret the chord outlined in bar 21 on beat 2 as a kind of A

---

[133] By the author.

major with an added minor ninth, the F sharp chord is established in the next bar. The line D sharp, E, F (!), E, D sharp, and D does mirror the harmonic strain and détente of the context, almost evoking the notion of a "banister" or a "garland".

Starting in bar 24, an unusual development occurs. In the upper-voice melodic sequence, a pattern of two bars is created. The ascending line of A sharp, B natural, and C corresponds to the following line in bar 28 et seqq. (C sharp, D, and E flat). The bass line, descending at first in reaction to the movements of interval of seconds (bar 24 et seqq.: B natural, B flat, A flat, and G) rises from bar 28 on, parallel to the upper voice. Syncopations, also used by Arnold, stress this rhythmic figure of the upper voice.[134] The middle voice, though, always moves around the tones of D and D sharp (*cf.* bar 24 et seqq.). Except for the single fifth leap in bar 29, the most striking feature of this passage is indeed its monotony. It is as if Arnold actually intended to draw out this moment in spite of its increasing harmonic tension. Since the rhythmic model remains the same, one almost has the impression of a complex and static model, creating an increasingly dramatic effect. The octavo leap of the middle voice in bar 31 and the descending melodic line that follows, in a contrary motion, almost evoke the notion of release.

In the following duets –duets in the truest sense of the word, a two-part texture in very different combinations,[135] often voiced in a very open structure with a large ambitus (*cf.* letter $\boxed{G}$ piccolo-flute and violas) – Arnold uses an extremely peculiar contrapuntal language. Quaver movements dominate, partially interrupted by the marginal use of a minim, the latter sometimes used as a syncopation on beat 3. Besides, almost exclusively, movements of the interval of seconds are applied. Indeed, Arnold interrupts this procedure at letter $\boxed{H}$. On a chromatic melodic surface, B flat, A, G sharp, F sharp, and E, elaborated with trills by the second violin, broken staccato triads and a D chromatic melody B flat, A, G sharp, G, F sharp fis, E, and D, which are combined in the second violin with trills and a staccato-articulation, broken triads (A flat major with added major seventh; G-sharp-minor seventh chord) occur, but this intermezzo is only barely developed. Immediately at letter $\boxed{J}$ Arnold returns to the duet structure, and only in $\boxed{M}$ and $\boxed{N}$ does this new element receive any acknowledgment.

These observations can lead to one conclusion. In contrast to many of his symphonies, in which he applied the sonata form and followed it to a certain extent, Arnold comes to a conclusion from his fantasy cycle for unaccompanied solo instruments, composed between 1967 and 1987. The principal subject played at the beginning of the movement can be understood as a kind of compositional column. Only in the beginning and at the end –in a manic-like gesture to be played extremely slowly (quaver equal to 96 MM) within the greatest possible orchestral tutti-scoring, *cf.*

---

[134] Later, at letter $\boxed{P}$, this syncopation becomes more important. Three trumpets must intonate, in *forte* and in their high range, these syncopations for a period of 20 bars (!).

[135] For a precise listing of the duets, see Jackson (JACKSON 2003:193).

allargando at letter $\boxed{I}$, does the subject occur. The rest of the time he falls back on an unfettered imagination and a freer concept of form while he concentrates on this column. Relationships to the subject within these free segments originate only by coincidence. Here, Arnold as a composer, confident in his own abilities, behaves for the first time according to the idealised image of the composer. He writes a work straight onto paper, so to speak. The fact that the particell shows no scratchings or corrections underscores this, as well.

However, we should *not* come to the conclusion that Arnold composed thoughtlessly or boringly, acting as a "geek". His concentration, shown in the act of composing, led to a work that was ahead of its time – comparable to Sibelius's 4th Symphony – a work that was just waiting for both an unprejudiced listener and a predetermined specialist. Simply ignoring Arnold's 9th Symphony would be wrong – these moments explicitly demand an analysis. In this sense, the annotator's remark, already quoted in context of Arnold's 2nd Symphony, shall be mentioned again, but now with an emphasis on Arnold's 9th: "...Let us hope the Symphony has the success it richly deserves, - British music will be all the better for that. If it were not for my inherent caution, I should be inclined to cry, 'Hats off, gentlemen!'..." (ANON. 1953:611).

181

7. Symphony No. 9: Reduction and Compositional Stringency

8. Stylistic Constants in Arnold's Work: A Summary. Musical Vocabulary, Form, Harmony, Melodic Invention, and Orchestration

"...Man könnte überhaupt die Frage stellen, ob es eine stilistisch reine Musik, die jeglicher Merkmale der Polystilistik entbehrt, gibt?...." Zofia Lissa *(LISSA 1973)*

"...One could generally ask whether is there a stylistically pure music which is without any sign of polystylistics?...."

Summarising the results of any scientific research clearly falls into the purvue of the current research canon. It rounds out a paper and recalls essential single phenomena that have been examined on a microcosmic level, considering them in a broader context (macrocosmic consideration).

Any analytic and aesthetic assessment must also be carried out carefully. On the one hand, in Arnold's particular case, the subject of research is in the difficult position of not being able to defend himself against any interpretation – remember, when Arnold was alive, he liked to attack his critics. On the other hand, it is difficult to generalise about a compositional personality: one cannot explain a complex, creative artist in a three-page summary.[136]

Altug Ünlü has, however, provided a systematic study of Gustav Mahler's orchestration technique (ÜNLÜ 2006) – and Schaarwächter did the same for the development of the British symphony from 1914 to 1945 (SCHAARWÄCHTER 1994). Both studies, however, in spite of their detailed perspectives, lack a real summary. The brevity of their endings leave the reader feeling that a true summing-up is completely absent.

Schaarwächter wrote a valuable source study, but his final summary diminished its overall effectiveness. Schaarwächter argued that in Britain there were, instead of an image of variety, clearly differentiated lines. He called these composers the „...formal akademischen...Komponisten, dann Komponisten, die durch Sibelius beeinflusst waren, zuletzt Komponisten der "Neuen Einfachheit"("formal or academic composers; composers influenced by Sibelius, and finally composers of the "new simplicity"). His argument is not plausible. Schaarwächter's statement, „...Die verschiedenen Richtungen der Gestaltung von Sinfonien bilden, gleichwohl ob in Großbritannien oder sonstwo (nur anderswo vielleicht nicht in ihrer ganzen Komplizität) ein klar gegliedertes Netzwerk..." (SCHAARWÄCHTER 1994:358) *("...The different directions of creating a symphony, whether in Great Britain or somewhere*

---

[136] Although there exists the so-called *Three-Page Sonata* by Charles Ives – but this is a side-issue!

else (but somewhere else not in their whole complexity), form a clear network ..."), must be viewed critically, even if we concede that in a final thesis there must be a necessary reduction. It is much too enticing to divide the world along clear lines – the musical world is much too diverse for such a division. Composers are unquestionably influenced by the works of their colleagues – both friends and those a composer finds odious – but, as a rule, they do not operate as a network. They insist on their independence and their singularity. The variety, not the conformity, of composition styles is what gives music its beauty. The author will take particular moments of Arnold's compositional technique, highlight the elements, and draw his conclusions from them. The author will also introduce two new terms that have not previously been used in research on Arnold: "Arnold's vocabulary" and "Arnoldian counterpoint".

8.1 Structure of Subjects, Syntax, and Form; Melodic Development

Arnold's saying, "to write a good tune" can be classified as a clear stylistic constant – obviously with a positive connotation. His subjects, mostly classically developed (antecedent-consequent structure), are usually designed to be lyrical and very song-like. The fact that Arnold uses certain compositional techniques, for example a sequence of motifs and rhythmic modification (repetition of a motif on another beat, often leading to the effect of a syncopation), is not unusual; nevertheless, two moments are still significant. On the one hand, Arnold tends to incorporate chord arpeggios into his melodies (*cf. The Concerto for Trumpet and Orchestra)*, and most of the final movements of his symphonies use fanfare-orientated melodic lines. Interestingly, Arnold often approaches the characteristic dissonance of the chord (usually not pure major or minor chords, but major-seventh or minor-seventh chords) and stresses its tension note by using larger note values, but generally compensates this upward movement by a following step-wise motion downward. One could describe this as the balancing of a ballistic curve (*Pace de la Motte!*).[137]

On the other hand, Arnold loves to approach target notes by using grace notes. This creates the impression of speech; one can almost imagine how a conductor could underline these "speaking" grace notes with a corresponding movement of his hand. However, these stylistic constants are not limited to his symphonic works; he applies them in his chamber music, as well (*cf. Sonata for Flute and Piano*, as well as the piano accompanying voice in his single song *Neglected*).

His use of intervals is not, in general, limited to specific intervals; he varies them according to the work and its overall need or intended expression. In works that have a dramatic expression, this is reflected by the use of certain intervallic movements – larger leaps that create a higher

---

[137] However, this is only the author's personal connotation.

degree of dissonance. One might think that Arnold's melodic development could be described as classicistic – remember Arnold's preference for the diatonic versus the chromatic. The basis for his melodic inventions is usually diatonically conceived; chromaticism is used to sharpen or to complement the melodic development. Because Arnold thinks in terms of "subjects" – in contrast to post-1945 avant-garde music as a whole – he has to think classicistically, i.e., subjects must have a certain course of development. As often stated, there are almost no scribbles in his sketches or final scores; therefore, we must regard his feel for periodicity and syntax in his tunes as a natural gift.

Critics have unilaterally overemphasised the simplicity of Arnold's subjects – the fact that Arnold's tunes are easy to memorise has been interpreted as a composer's aesthetic mistake. Instead, this in fact makes Arnold's subjects authentic. The question of a composer's authenticity must not be forgotten, as it is important to any judgement. Adorno has apparently provided a clear criteria in his Aesthetic Theory: „...Die authentische Kunst der Vergangenheit, die derzeit sich verhüllen muß, ist dadurch nicht gerichtet. Die großen Werke warten. Etwas von ihrem Wahrheitsgehalt zergeht nicht mit dem metaphysischen Sinn, so wenig es sich festnageln läßt; es ist das, wodurch sie beredt bleiben.... Was einmal in einem Kunstwerk wahr gewesen ist und durch den Gang der Geschichte dementiert ward, vermag erst dann wieder sich zu öffnen, wenn die Bedingungen verändert sind, um derentwillen jene Wahrheit kassiert werden mußte: so tief sind ästhetisch Wahrheitsgehalt und Geschichte ineinander. Die versöhnte Realität und die wiederhergestellte Wahrheit am Vergangenen dürften miteinander konvergieren. Was an vergangener Kunst noch erfahrbar ist und von Interpretation zu erreichen, ist wie eine Anweisung auf einen solchen Zustand. Nichts verbürgt, daß sie real honoriert werde. Die Tradition ist nicht abstrakt zu negieren, sondern unnaiv nach dem gegenwärtigen Stand zu kritisieren: so konstituiert das Gegenwärtige das Vergangene. Nichts ist unbesehen, nur weil es vorhanden ist und einst etwas galt, zu übernehmen, nichts aber auch erledigt, weil es verging; Zeit allein ist kein Kriterium. Ein unabsehbarer Vorrat von Vergangenem erweist immanent sich als unzulänglich, ohne daß die betroffenen Gebilde es an Ort und Stelle und fürs Bewußtsein ihrer eigenen Periode gewesen wären. Die Mängel werden durch den zeitlichen Verlauf demaskiert... Nur das je Fortgeschrittenste hat Chance gegen den Zerfall in der Zeit. Im Nachleben der Werke jedoch werden qualitative Differenzen offenbar, die keineswegs mit dem Grad an Modernität zu ihrer Periode koinzidieren. In dem geheimen bellum omnium contra omnes, das die Geschichte der Kunst erfüllt, mag als Vergangenes das ältere Moderne über das neuere siegen. Nicht daß eines Tages das par ordre du jour Altmodische sich als dauerhafter, gediegener bewähren könnte als das Avancierte. Hoffnung auf Renaissancen der Pfitzner und Sibelius, der Carossa oder Hans Thoma sagen mehr über die, welche sie hegen, als über die Wertbeständigkeit von derlei Seele....“ (ADORNO 2003:3826ff [cf. GS 7, S. 67 ff.])

"...History's true art, necessarily concealed at present, remains thus undirected. Great works lie in wait. Something of their internal truth remains in a metaphysical sense, so much as it can be pinpointed; and that is why they continue to be discussed... The truth that was once seen in an aesthetic work and consequently denied over the course of history, can only be brought to light once circumstances have changed, for it was due to those circumstances that such truth had to be rejected – that is how interwoven internal truth and history are in terms of aesthetics. Reconciled reality and reconstructed truth of the past ought to converge. Experiencing historical art, we are still able to interpret from it as pointing towards such a situation. Nothing guarantees that it will actually be honoured. The traditional cannot be abstractly denied, instead it must be criticised according to the present situation, thus the past is constituted by the present. Nothing is unobserved purely because of its existence and because in former times it meant something to pass on the tradition, nothing is settled because it is past; time alone is not a criterion. History's endless store proves immanently inadequate, without the creations themselves being right there and aware of their own epoch. Inadequacies are revealed over the course of time... Only the most advanced has a chance against the decay of time. These works live on, yet qualitative differences are apparent, which in no way coincide with their epoch's degree of modernity. In the hidden bellum omnium contra omnes, *as represented by the history of art, the older modernity may triumph over the more recent in forming the past. Not that the* par-ordre-du-jour *antiquated modernity could ever supersede the more recent as the longer lasting and superior. Hope for the renaissance of Pfitzner and Sibelius, of Carossa or Hans Thoma says more about those who hold out for it than about the lasting worthiness of those gentlemen...".*

The thesis that Adorno probably would have devalued Arnold (as in Sibelius's case) is put forth, and is not far-fetched. However, Adorno's theses suffer because they always set out explicit requirements for the authenticity of a piece of art – they do not evaluate deviations in relative terms but rather consider them an offence, a memory of the past, or even reactionary, always with a negative connotation. Authenticity, for Adorno, requires an awareness of the past (*cf.* Eggebrecht's earlier claim concerning tradition) but a heedless belief in progress itself. One can use compositional techniques from the past, but must always take into account their saturation – otherwise one shall always prefer more contemporary techniques. Adorno would have interpreted Arnold's subjects in as banal a fashion as he did Mahler's. However, in contrast to Schönberg, who finally evaluated Mahler's subjects as more profound than they had previously been deemed, Adorno would hardly have conceded that Arnold intended to "unmask" the saturation of his subjects by writing them in a saturated manner. Arnold does not think in categories. For him, music is primarily a feeling, a way of expressing thoughts and emotions, and that feeling is clearly intended to be shared by the listener. Therefore, the tune-like nature of his melodies is definitely a means of achieving this interaction with the listener.

In writing about contemporary composers, Whittall has repeatedly used the concept of a composer as a "modern classicist" and has proved through his arguments how this can be applied to, for instance, Maxwell Davies (WHITTALL 1997:144-146).[138] Indeed, the author suggests that this concept can also be applied to Malcolm Arnold, because the concept does not have as negative a connotation as the concept of "serious" and "light" composers. Whittall's concept fits Arnold very well in terms of his compositional criteria. He subjects classicistic elements such as harmony, melodic development, the use of conventional topoi, and form/syntax to a modernistic perception – but not in the sense of *Gebrauchsmusik*. Rather, the elements are perceived as artificial pieces of art. The context of Arnold's tune-like subjects must be considered, revealing the true compositional and aesthetic value of his compositions. An adequate research work about Arnold should consider not only (for example) the interval of a major third, but must perceive the larger image, or context. Only then will Arnold's modern classicism – not to be confused with the negatively perceived concept of neoclassicism in musical composition – and his singularity as a composer become visible.

8.2 The Craft of Musical Composition

8.2.1 Compositional Structures

Arnold's preferred compositional structures shall now be quickly enumerated. A three-layer model dominates (melody, harmonic accompaniment layer, and if necessary a contrapuntal layer as a supplement); this has been examined in depth in this study. If this model is used, we can speak in general of the primacy of the melody.[139]

There is an ever-increasing contrast between these three layers and Arnold's preference for pure two-part writing. Very suddenly, his musical structure becomes thinner, and, particularly in his orchestral symphonic works, Arnold does not shy away from pairing together the most different musical instruments in his two-part counterpoint.

This particular phenomena can be classified by introducing the term "Arnoldian counterpoint", as mentioned earlier. This concept should by no means be considered exclusive to Arnold, as it is also common in the music-theoretical considerations of Renaissance music (often described as "Palestrinian counterpoint") or baroque music ("Bach counterpoint"). In

---

[138] Whittall also uses the concept in relation to Sibelius (WHITTALL 2004:64f).

[139] Ünlü had examined this concept in terms of instrumentation – it does not concern the melodic development.

contrast to Renaissance music, basically all contrapuntal devices and all possible combinations of intervals are available to Arnold – there is, for example, no specific rule for an appropriate resolution of a syncopation dissonance as there is in Renaissance music. However, Arnold prefers, in his more expressive opuses, a very special contrapuntal voice; he places the emphasis on the dissonance itself or on the implied dissonant harmonic progression. The two voice duets of his 9th Symphony can be cited as an example. The *Four Irish Dances* (cf. chapter on the myth of invention), and above all the slow movement, also indicate that Arnold emphasises vertically dissonant harmonies. They are, in fact, not just emphasised, but in some places vehemently turned into absurdities through the repetition of the same two-part harmony over and over again. A composer writing dissonant counterpoint is not unusual. Nevertheless, the absurdity itself is why it is justifiable to introduce the term "Arnoldian counterpoint" – and not to speak of an pastiche-like Shostakovitchian counterpoint. Though Arnold knew Shostakovitch personally and admired his music (HARRIS/MEREDITH 2004: 228ff), the existing research on Arnold has often tried to articulate a closeness to Shostakovitch, in particular Burton-Page (BURTON-PAGE 1989:42;77;99;111;122;127). Regarding the more dissonant counterpoint style, we must still admit that Arnold's counterpoint, despite its similarity to Shostakovitch's, has a much thinner texture and is not as interwoven as it is in Shostakovitch's case. Therefore the author recommends differentiating between these two composers rather than grouping Arnold with Shostakovitch.

Arnold's dissonant two-part writing does not originate from a similarly unilateral dissonant horizontal consecutive order of intervals, but is limited to the vertical level. Thus, some Arnoldian counterpoint from his late works initially evokes the notion that he did not pay enough attention to the consonance degree of the voice-leading. In fact, the opposite is true. This more dissonant Arnoldian counterpoint is conscious, and belongs therefore to Arnold's normative vocabulary. Unlike the superficial perception of the style it suggests (i.e., "Arnoldish"), he is not a composer of "light" music that is full of consonances. The misunderstanding of his style results from the fact that commentators primarily refer to his music for special occasions (e.g., the *English Dances* or his film music). The dissonant facet of his personality, which can be found, for instance, in most of his chamber music (*cf.* also the sombre *Sonata for Violin and Piano*) must be included in the overall image of Arnold.

Another compositional element, the ostinato, should also not be forgotten. Above all, Arnold's symphonic works always show ostinato structures, usually the two-bar harmonic progressions that he uses in his dances. But the rhythmic ostinati are also a sign of Arnold's personal style. In that respect, Sibelius's influence is immanently noticeable. The ostinato represents the most rudimentary form of repetition and creates a musical context in which fragments of the subjects are "thrown in". Indeed,

Arnold pays tribute to Sibelius's compositional technique without literally copying it.

All these compositional means, viewed as a whole, represent Arnold's unique style and make his music immediately identifiable. The reason he almost never had to "sketch out" these means is also evident; they belong to his vocabulary. Of course, all composers are free to make use of these same means and procedures. however, Arnold's particular selection of means forms his vocabulary. To him, they were so natural that he did not even talk about them, regarding it as "donkey-work". He is in complete command of his musical and compositional language – therefore the author strongly encourages the scientific community to pass along his term vocabulary.

8.2.2 Harmony

It is dangerous to reduce the harmonic thinking of a composer; an analysis must present much more than a statistical argument. In Arnold's case, however, it is remarkable that the minor-seventh chord and the major-seventh chord are constants in his style. They appear in his earliest compositions as well as in his late works.

In addition, Arnold understands how to aggravate these "basis chords" with numerous characteristic dissonances (chord tensions), even distorting the chords to a point where they are unrecognisable. Nevertheless, in this respect he does not follow a higher compositional principle. If, for example, close clusters of seconds appear (*cf. Mylady* in the sketches for *The Three Musketeers*), these are reduced for other reasons. Arnold's chord language is multifaceted and diverse; all possible voicing positions and structures (closed/open position) are applied and the application of these is in no way made systematic.

Arnold does not use the relationship of keys in a textbook-like manner. Arnold prefers modulatory processes to mediant-related keys, often reaching them by means of enharmonic leading tone procedures. However, at the same time he is not afraid of modulating to the most unrelated tonal region (remember the tritone constellation of his 2nd Symphony). Modulations are rarely caused purely formally by Arnold, i.e., they are not coupled with the introduction of a new subject. They derive from the melodic strivings of the compositions. The chord progressions of *Homage to the Queen* (*cf.* chapter 5) are a very impressive example of this.

The layering of chords or harmonies, often implying polytonality, is yet another element of Arnold's style (*cf.* 6th Symphony). Therefore, very close layers of chords are preferred (as, for example, E major/B major), resulting in clashes of inside intervals. Arnold likes to use these polytonal chords as background pads (surfaces), often scored to the low brass section and sometimes even combined with a structural function (polytonal blocks, *cf.* analysis of the 6th Symphony). It is interesting that this procedure can also be found in Sibelius's 4th Symphony, in which harmonic blocks in the brass section also appear as functional transitional material, though they are substantially less dissonantly conceived.

However, it is particularly noticeable that the harmony in Arnold's film music is much less complex than in his concertante symphonic oeuvre. This may have something to do with the special requirements for film music in Great Britain. Still, the basic chords that Arnold favoured can always be found. A beautiful example is the lyrical main theme of *Whistle Down the Wind*, which creates an almost jazz-like feel with its ostinato seventh-chord accompaniment.

8.3. *Instrumentation*

Arnold's orchestration skills have been regarded as brilliant and extremely capable by various authors who have already been mentioned. His orchestration reveals transparency, consists of widespread extremes of orchestral colours, and skillfully uses orchestral instruments. This is in contrast to the usual pompous British orchestration from about 1900 to the 1950's. Schaarwächter pointed out that Gordon Jacob (1895-1894), Arnold's composition teacher at the Royal College of Music, applied a similarly transparent but equally virtuosic orchestration technique in his works, not corresponding to the norm at that time: "...Neben Adrian Boult, Herbert Howells und George Thalben Ball gehörte Gordon Percival Septimus Jacob...zu den langjährigen Dozenten am Royal College of Music....Er war als außerordentlich bescheidener Dozent geschätzt und beliebt,....obgleich er von seinen Kollegen Dyson und Howells nicht die angemessene Anerkennung erhielt, vielleicht weil ihm der Ruch des Gelegenheitskomponisten anhaftete und weil seine eigene äußere klare Instrumentation, die stets mit dem Notwendigen auskam, aber nie in Klangfarben schwelgte, nicht gar zu sehr nach dem Geschmack seiner Kollegen war...Jacobs Schwierigkeit lag, abgesehen davon, dass er sich nicht mehr die instrumentationstechnischen Neuerungen Schönbergs und Weberns aneignete (was ihn jedoch für zahlreiche seiner Zetigenossen, allen voran V. Williams, zum optimalen Berater in orchestrationstechnischen Fragen machte, ihm jedoch Einfluss wie den Richard Halls versagte) jedoch darin, dass seine Musik beim Publikum nicht die nachhaltige elektrisierende Wirkung auszulösen imstande war, die vonnöten ist, um sich einen Platz im Herzen des Zuhörers zu sichern..." (SCHAARWÄCHTER 1994:72–73).

("... Besides Adrian Boult, Herbert Howells and George Thalben Ball, Gordon Percival Septimus Jacob...was one of the long-standing lecturers at the Royal College of Music....He was liked as an exceptionally modest lecturer...although he did not receive adequate recognition from his colleagues Dyson and Howells, maybe because they saw him as a composer of works for special occasions and because his extremely transparent orchestration, which always applied only the necessary but never indulged itself in effects, was not very much to his colleagues' taste...Nevertheless, Jacob's difficulty lay, apart from the fact that he did

190

not adopt any new orchestration techniques invented by Schönberg and Webern (which made him the optimal adviser for numerous contemporaries, especially V. Williams, in orchestration questions, but at the same prevented him from enjoying more influence like Richard Hall), in the fact that his music did not create the lasting, electrifying effect that is necessary to earn a place in the listener's heart...").

Schaarwächter's evaluation of the missing "electrifying" effect in Jacob's orchestral music must be seen as a subjective judgement. However, it is probably not wrong to suppose Jacob's orchestration technique influenced Arnold, because Arnold very much liked his former teacher. Further, Jacob's *Orchestral Technique: A Manual for Students* is still one of the standard English orchestration textbooks.

We can demonstrate Arnold's tendency to use bright and widespread sounds through his own statement (his remark that he abhors the English horn as an instrument is also quite amusing): "...I think that, in augmenting the orchestra, composers have been sadly led astray. They usually add instruments to the middle of the orchestra, already the heaviest part, with 'cellos, violas, horns, bassoons, clarinets and trombones. They add cor anglais or bass clarinet or saxophone. The extremes are the areas that want augmenting, to enrich the colour and add vitality. The instruments needed are: extra flutes, piccolos, E-flat clarinet, contra-bassoon. I've never used a cor anglais in my life..." (SCHAFER 1963:148).

His statements are clearly demonstrated by his entire oeuvre. The woodwinds are often used in their high register and the brass section often intonates chord layers in a low register, reminding one of Berlioz and creating Arnold's typical expressivity.

Nevertheless, the unique quality of Arnold's orchestration skills is, in the truest sense of the word, his perfect knowledge of the instruments. This perfection has both positive and negative implications. We must first define what (in general) a perfect orchestration is. Arnold uses instruments archetypally and emphasises their strengths; the vital and agile instruments (strings and woodwind instruments) are provided with particularly agile passages (fast runs, etc.). One tendency is clearly recognisable: Arnold orchestrates his symphonic music in an almost textbook-like manner. That statement is not, however, intended to carry its usual negative connotation. Arnold's orchestration skills did delight the audience, but, more importantly, they were also pleasing to the orchestral musicians. The musicians were not unchallenged, but neither were they overly stressed to the very edge of their abilities. The virtuosity and meaningfulness of orchestral effects are always well balanced. There are hardly any passages in Arnold's symphonic music in which structures cover each other up; they always blend well.

A negative result, however, is that Arnold does not avoid the extreme ranges of the instruments – remember the lyrical bassoon entry of the subject in the third movement of his 2nd Symphony. However, the high register is seldom used to its absolute extreme. Arnold's orchestration appears, in particular during the years of his most creative period in the fifties and sixties, to be archetypal. Figuratively speaking, the instruments "speak" in the way one expects them to speak; it almost seems that Arnold has taken lessons in orchestration from Prokofieff. One vainly searches for a tantalising bassoon audition piece, as in Stravinsky's *Sacre du Printemps*. Perhaps numerous contemporaries would have seen Arnold from a different perspective if he had dared to go further in this context. Indeed, we shall not forget that his famous and virtuosic brass pieces have made a major contribution to brass literature – the brass instruments are not used for chordic or chorale-like effects. His first quintet for brass is still a landmark piece, demanding virtuosity and lyrical playing at the same time.

If we now look at the orchestration technique in Arnold's late works, it is even more astonishing that his 9th Symphony has not received the acknowledgment which it would seem to have earned. Since Arnold is in his element, aiming straight for the orchestral/instrumental extremes, this piece demands further analysis. The orchestration of the 9th Symphony is marked by a fascinating transparency, displaying wide extremes in terms of orchestration. In contrast to Arnold's earlier pompous orchestral "fireworks", his 9th Symphony seems almost thin. The fact that this simplicity is not interpreted by commentators and music analysts as kind of a Webernian brilliance is ironic. Instead, they still apply existing explanation patterns, categorising Arnold as a successor to Berlioz, Sibelius, or Mahler. Let us hope that future studies will illuminate this same point.

In conclusion, Arnold's orchestration technique can be described as very flexible in terms of its adaptation. His colour palette is enormously multifaceted – indeed, normative, but not dogmatic. Arnold remained, throughout his life, not just a composer, but, in his way of thinking, an instrumentalist. His understanding, which he expressed in 1956, that instrumentalists, just like composers, want their best to be demanded, but not over-demanded (ARNOLD 1956:168f), is his credo throughout his life. It finally leads to a noteworthy confluence between the composer and his personality.

8.4 Summary and Review

Arnold's symphonic works offer many surprises and peculiarities, but also normative constants and conventions. This study could not, of course, analyse each of Arnold's works, but this selection of works reveals noteworthy qualities of Arnold's compositional style, showing a remarkable consistency – but also consistent development. We may not agree with every music-analytical consideration; nevertheless, something has become evident in an aesthetic sense. Adorno's demand for the authenticity of a composer pertains to Arnold in a very unconventional way. In his compositional aesthetic, Arnold orientates himself towards certain models without losing his own voice; bear in mind that he had to work from, and within, an isolated position in the English contemporary music movement. One more thing must still be noted. Arnold's works are authentic in and of themselves. His works show polystylistic influences, he pursues his own, internal goals instead of adapting contemporary tendencies, and he has an unmistakeable style that is expressed throughout his entire symphonic oeuvre and cannot be reduced to a minor selection of well-known popular opuses. It is astonishing that the term "Arnoldish" still exists, regardless of whether it is used positively or negatively. We should begin to understand Arnold as a composer of high aesthetic value, and this can only be done through critical and music-theoretical analysis. Calling him, on the one hand, "Britain's most misunderstood composer" or labelling him "The Brilliant and the Dark" is correct. On the other hand, we will only find the singularity of Arnold's music if we approach it auditively **and** analytically. If we leave aside aesthetic considerations, we can forget stereotypes and will not reduce Arnold to a composer of masterly "tunes". If we examine his music by arguing compositionally as well as analytically, we will see his symphonic writing as a whole and we can then position him clearly in the context of contemporary music.

Arnold's extremely demanding oeuvre, in which he combines orchestral brilliance with his sense of syntactic compositional unity, easily overcomes the prejudicial barriers of serious and light music. Perhaps Arnold's life is portrayed in his works like no other British composer's. Arnold's music is full of energy, but can turn lightness into the deepest melancholy; its musical intensity makes it almost impossible not to be touched by it. His compositions underline the charisma of his personality. It is your turn, Sir Malcolm, the *grandseigneur* of British music: "When I am asked to write music for ballet, a school orchestra, a film or a revue, I write exactly what I would like to hear if I were to go to the particular entertainment for which the music has been commissioned. On quite a number of occasions, my ideas have coincided with other people's – from which you will gather that my stars have been lucky indeed!" (ARNOLD 1956:168f).

8. Stylistic Constants in Arnold's Work: A Summary. Musical Vocabulary, Form, Harmony, Melodic Invention, and Orchestration

9. Bibliography

Abraham, Gerald (ed.) (1947): The music of Sibelius. New York: Norton.

Adorno, Theodor W.; Tiedemann, Rolf; Adorno, Gretel (2003): Theodor W. Adorno, gesammelte Schriften. Berlin. Directmedia-Publ. (Reihe Digitale Bibliothek, Teil 97).

___ (2006 [1947]): Philosophy of new music. Translated, Edited and with an introduction by Robert Hullot-Kentor. Minneapolis: University of Minnesota Press.

Anderson, Julian (2004): Sibelius and contemporary music. In: Grimley, Daniel M. (ed.): The Cambridge Companion to Sibelius. Cambridge: Cambridge Univ. Press.

Angerer, Manfred (1984): Musikalischer Ästhetizismus, analytische Studien zu Skrjabins Spätwerk. Tutzing. Schneider (Reihe Wiener Veröffentlichungen zur Musikwissenschaft, Teil 23).

___ (1994): Ironisierung der Konvention und humoristische Totalität. Über die ersten Takte von Gustav Mahlers IV. Symphonie. Vergleichend-systematische Musikwissenschaft, p. 561–582.

___ (1998): Zukunft muss ermöglicht werden. ÖMZ, 53. Jg, Nr. 10, p. 35–43.

___ (2006): Gestrichener Kanon. Einleitende Bemerkungen zu Anspruch und Geltung, zu Mythologie und Lokaltradition der Gattung Streichquartett. In: Angerer, Manfred; Ottner, Carmen; Rathgeber, Eike (ed.): Musikalische Gesprächskultur. Das Streichquartett im habsburgischen Vielvölkerstaat. Symposium 25.-27. April 2002. Wien. Doblinger. Beiträge der Österreichischen Gesellschaft für Musik, p. 8–15.

Angerer, Manfred; Ottner, Carmen; Rathgeber, Eike (ed.) (2006): Musikalische Gesprächskultur. Das Streichquartett im habsburgischen Vielvölkerstaat. Symposium 25.-27. April 2002. Wien. Doblinger (Reihe Beiträge der Österreichischen Gesellschaft für Musik, Teil 12).

Anon. (1953): Reviews of new music. Scores. In: Musical Opinion, Volume 65, July 1953. Bournemouth, Bourne Press. p. 611.

Anon. (2004): Sir Malcolm Arnold. The complete catalogue of published works. London. Available at Novello.

Arnold, Malcolm (1956): I think of music in terms of sounds. Nachgedruckt in: Burton-Page, Piers. (1994): Philharmonic Concerto. London. Methuen, p.166-169.

___ (1971): Don't shoot the pianist. Reprinted in: Burton-Page, Piers. (1994): Philharmonic Concerto. London. Methuen, p.169ff.

Bach, E.p. (1991): A performance project on selected works of five composers. D.M.A. dissertation, University of British Columbia (Canada).

Bacharach, A. L. (ed.) (1951): British Music of our time. Harmondsworth, Middlesex: Penguin Books.

Baggini, Julian; Stangroom, Jeremy (ed.) (2002): New British Philosophy. The Interviews. London. Routledge.

Benson, Bruce E. (2003): The Improvisation of Musical Dialogue: A Phenomenology of Music. Cambridge. Cambridge University Press.

Bürger, Peter (1974): Theorie der Avantgarde. Frankfurt. suhrkamp.

Burton-Page, Piers. (1994): Philharmonic Concerto. London. Methuen.

Cassirer, Ernst [1944] (2000): Versuch über den Menschen. Einführung in eine Philosophie der Kunst (1944). In: Schüßler, Werner (ed.): Philosophische Anthropologie. Freiburg. Alber. Alber-Texte Philosophie, p. 108–125.

Cherniavsky, David (1947): Special Characteristics of Sibelius's Style. In: Abraham, Gerald (ed.): The music of Sibelius. New York: Norton, p. 141–176.

Chua, Daniel K. L. (1999): Absolute music and the construction of meaning. Cambridge. Cambridge Univ. Press (Reihe New perspectives in music history and criticism).

Cole, Hugo (1989): Malcolm Arnold. An Introduction to his Music. London. Faber and Faber.

Cook, Nicholas; Pople, Anthony (2004): The Cambridge history of twentieth-century music. Cambridge. Cambridge University Press.

Craggs, Stewart R. (1998): Malcolm Arnold. A Bio-Bibliography. Westport; London. Greenwood Press (Reihe Bio-Bibliographies in Music, no, Teil 69).

Danuser, Hermann; Katzenberger, Günter (ed.) (1993): Vom Einfall zum Kunstwerk. Der Kompositionsprozess in der Musik des 20. Jahrhunderts. Laaber: Laaber (4).

Danuser, Hermann (ed.) (1997): Die klassizistische Moderne in der Musik des 20. Jahrhundert. Internationales Symposium der Paul Sacher Stiftung Basel 1996. Basel: Amadeus Verlag (Veröffentlichungen der Paul Sacher Stiftung Band, 5).

Dibelius, Ulrich (1998): Moderne Musik nach 1945. München. Piper.

Eagleton, Terry (1984): The Function of Criticism. London. Verso.

___ (1990): The Ideology of the Aesthetic. Oxford. Blackwell.

___ [1983[1]] (1996): Literary Theory. An Introduction. Second Edition. Minneapolis. University of Minnesota Press (reprint).

___ (1996): The Illusions of Postmodernism. Oxford. Blackwell.

___ (2003): After Theory. London. Penguin Books.

Eco, Umberto [1973] (1977): Das offene Kunstwerk. Frankfurt: suhrkamp, (suhrkamp taschenbuch wissenschaft).

Eco, Umberto (2003): Kant und das Schnabeltier. München: Dt. Taschenbuch-Verl.

Eco, Umberto; Schick, Walter [1977] (2005[11]): Wie man eine wissenschaftliche Abschlussarbeit schreibt. Doktor-, Diplom- und

Magisterarbeit in den Geistes- und Sozialwissenschaften. Heidelberg.
Müller (Reihe UTB für Wissenschaft; Interdisziplinär, Teil 1512).

Eggebrecht, Hans Heinrich (1999): Musikalisches Denken.
Aufsätze zur Theorie und Ästhetik in der Musik. Wilhelmshaven. Florian
Noetzel.

Eichel, Christine (1994): Von einem, der auszog, die Theorie
ästhetisch werden zu lassen. Adornos Ästhetik zwischen Begriffsterror und
Metaphernklang. In: Kolleritsch, Otto (ed.): Klischee und Wirklichkeit in
der Musikalischen Moderne. Wien. Universal Edition. Studien zur
Wertungsforschung, p. 159–173.

Evans, Peter (1979): The Music of Benjamin Britten. London. J.
M. Dent & Sons Limited.

Floros, Constantin (1985): Gustav Mahler. Band III Die
Symphonien. Wiesbaden: Breitkopf und Härtel.

Franklin, Peter (2004): Sibelius in Britain. In: Grimley, Daniel
M. (ed.): The Cambridge Companion to Sibelius. Cambridge: Cambridge
Univ. Press, p. 182–195.

Fuhr, Michael (2007): Populäre Musik und Ästhetik. Die
historisch-philosophische Rekonstruktion einer Geringschätzung.
Bielefeld: transcript Verlag (texte zur populären musik, 3).

G-F.,C. (1960): B.B.C. Symphony Orchestra. In: Musical
Opinion, 84 (December 1960). Bournemouth. Bourne Press. p. 143-144.

Gadamer, Hans-Georg [1960] (1990[6]): Hermeneutik I. Wahrheit
und Methode. Grundzüge e. philosoph. Hermeneutik. Tübingen. Mohr
(Reihe Gesammelte Werke, Teil 1).

Garnham, A. M. (2003): Hans Keller and the BBC. The musical
conscience of British broadcasting 1959-79. Hants: Ashgate.

Goehr, Lydia (1992): The Imaginary Museum of Musical Works.
An Essay in the Philosophy of Music. Oxford. Clarendon Press.

Grimley, Daniel M. (ed.) (2004): The Cambridge Companion to
Sibelius. Cambridge: Cambridge Univ. Press.

Groth, Renate (1993): Claude Debussy. "Ein bisschen vom
Geheimnis bewahren". In: Danuser, Hermann; Katzenberger, Günter (ed.):
Vom Einfall zum Kunstwerk. Der Kompositionsprozess in der Musik des
20. Jahrhunderts. Laaber: Laaber 4), p. 23–34.

Hanna, S.R (1993): Analysis and performance of music for
unaccompanied bassoon by Malcolm Arnold, Gordon Jacob, William
Osborne, George Perle and Vincent Persichetti. D.M.A Eastman School of
Music, University of Rochester, New York.

Harris, Paul; Meredith, Anthony (2004): Malcolm Arnold: Rogue
Genius. The Life and Music of Britain's most misunderstood composer.
Norwich. Thames/Elkin.

Heldt, Guido (2003): Erste Symphonien - Britten, Walton und
Tippett. In: Osthoff, Wolfgang; Schubert, Giselher (ed.): Symphonik 1930-
1950. Gattungsgeschichtliche und analytische Beiträge. Mainz: Schott, p.
84–108.

Hesse, Lutz-Werner (1983): Studien zum Schaffen des
Komponisten Ralph Vaughan Williams. Regensburg. Gustav Bosse Verlag
(Reihe Kölner Beiträge zur Musikforschung, Teil 134).

Hiekel, Jörn P. (2006): Musik inszeniert. Präsentation und Vermittlung zeitgenössischer Musik heute. Mainz: Schott.

Hirdina, Karin; Reschke, Renate (ed.) (2004): Ästhetik. Aufgabe(n) einer Wissenschaftsdisziplin. Freiburg. Rombach Verlag (Reihe Rombach Wissenschaften Reihe Litterae, Teil 120).

Hobsbawm, Eric (ed.) (2003): The invention of tradition. Cambridge: Cambridge Univ. Press (Canto).

___ (2003): Introduction: Inventing Traditions. In: Hobsbawm, Eric (ed.): The invention of tradition. Cambridge: Cambridge Univ. Press (Canto, p. 1–14.

Hofacre, M. J. (1986): The use of tenor trombone in 20th century brass quintet music. D.M.A. dissertation, University of Oklahoma.

Howell, Tim (2001): "Sibelius the Progressive". In: Jackson, Timothy L.; Murtomäki, Veijo (ed.): Sibelius studies. Cambridge: Cambridge Univ. Press, p. 35–57.

Howes, Frank (1974): The Music of William Walton. Oxford. Oxford University Press.

Huber, Nikolaus A. (1998): Erfahrungen mit Fortschritt. In: Metzger, H.-K.; Riehn, R. (ed.): Was heißt Fortschritt? München. edition text + kritik. Musik-Konzepte, p. 37–38.

Hull, Robin (1951): 'What Now?'. In: Bacharach, A. L. (ed.): British Music of our time. Harmondsworth, Middlesex: Penguin Books, p. 212–227.

Husserl, Edmund [1929] (1981²): Formale und transzendentale Logik (1929). Tübingen. Max Niemeyer Verlag.

Ingarden, Roman [1931] (1972): Das literarische Kunstwerk. Mit einem Anhang von den Funktionen der Sprache im Theaterschauspiel. Tübingen. Niemeyer.

Jackson, Paul R. W. (2003): The Life and Music of Sir Malcolm Arnold. The Brilliant and the Dark. Aldershot. Ashgate.

Jackson, Timothy L.; Murtomäki, Veijo (ed.) (2001): Sibelius studies. Cambridge: Cambridge Univ. Press.

Jost, Peter (2004): Instrumentation. Geschichte und Wandel des Orchesterklanges. Kassel. Bärenreiter (Reihe Bärenreiter-Studienbücher Musik, Teil 13).

Jungheinrich, Hans-Klaus (1998): Der Musikroman. Ein anderer Blick auf die Symphonie. Salzburg und Wien: Residenz Verlag.

Kandinsky, Wassily (1912): Über das Geistige in der Kunst. München. Piper & Co.

Kant, Immanuel; Weischedel, Wilhelm [1790] (1995): Kritik der Urteilskraft (1790). Frankfurt am Main. Suhrkamp (Reihe Suhrkamp-Taschenbuch Wissenschaft, Teil 10).

Karolyi, Otto (1994): Modern British Music. The Second British Musical Renaissance - From Elgar to P. Maxwell Davies. London. Associated University Presses.

Keller, Hans (1956): The New in Review. Malcolm Arnold (and Alan Hoddinott). In: Music Review, Ausgabe 17 (November 1956), p. 333-335.

___ (2001): Functional Analysis: The Unity of Contrasting Themes. Complete Editions of the Analytical Scores. Oxford: Peter Lang.

Kennedy, Michael (1989): Portrait of Walton. Oxford. Oxford University Press.

Kildea, Paul (2002): Selling Britten. Music and the Market Place. Oxford. Oxford University Press.

Kolleritsch, Otto (ed.) (1981): Zur "Neuen Einfachheit" in der Musik. Wien. Universal Edition (Reihe Studien zur Wertungsforschung Universität für Musik und darstellende Kunst, Teil 14).

___ (1994): Klischee und Wirklichkeit in der Musikalischen Moderne. Wien. Universal Edition (Reihe Studien zur Wertungsforschung, Teil 28).

Konrad, Ulrich (1992): Mozart's Sketches. Early Music, Jg. XX, p. 119–132.

Küng, Hans (2006): Musik und Religion. Mozart - Wagner - Bruckner. Frankfurt: Piper.

Lissa, Zofia (1973): Musikalisches Geschichtsbewusstsein - Segen oder Fluch? In: Stephan, Rudolf (ed.): Zwischen Tradition und Fortschritt. Über das musikalische Geschichtsbewusstsein. Mainz. Schott. Veröffentlichungen des Instituts für neue Musik und Musikerziehung Darmstadt, p. 9–30.

Loewe, Frederick (1969): My Fair Lady. Vocal Score revised version 1969. New York: Hal Leonard.

Matthus, Siegfried (1993): Der schöpferische Akt des Komponierens. Eine Selbstbefragung. In: Danuser, Hermann; Katzenberger, Günter (ed.): Vom Einfall zum Kunstwerk. Der Kompositionsprozess in der Musik des 20. Jahrhunderts. Laaber: Laaber 4), p. 395–411.

Mauser, Siegfried (ed.) (2002): Die Symphonie im 19. und 20. Jahrhundert. Unter Mitarbeit von W. Steinbeck und Chr. v. Blumröder. Laaber: Laaber.

Metzger, H.-K.; Riehn, R. (ed.) (1998): Was heißt Fortschritt? München. edition text + kritik (Reihe Musik-Konzepte, Teil 100).

Mitchell, Donald (1954): Some first performances. In: The Musical Times, Jg. 95, p. 382.

Morin, Alexander J. (2002): Classical Music: Third Ear. The Essential Listening Companion. San Fransisco: Backbeat Books.

Moseler, Günter (2002): Regionalisierung und Transformation der Form: Die englische Symphonie im 20. Jahrhundert. In: Mauser, Siegfried (ed.): Die Symphonie im 19. und 20. Jahrhundert. Laaber: Laaber, p. 194–207.

Nixon, David (2006): Autumn/Winter 2006 brochure Northern Ballet Theatre, Nottingham.

O'Brien, Monica (2005): Bombed-Out Consciousness: The negative Teleology of the Modern Subject in Adorno, Beckett and Delillo. Dissertation. Supervised by Levinson, Brinkler-Gabler, Spanos, Pensky. New York. Binghampton University State University of New York, Graduate School. Online at www.libumi.com/dissertations, UMI Number: 3164708.

Osthoff, Wolfgang; Schubert, Giselher (ed.) (2003): Symphonik 1930-1950. Gattungsgeschichtliche und analytische Beiträge. Mainz: Schott.

Pinder, Brigitte (2005): Form und Inhalt der symphonischen Tondichtungen von Sibelius. Probleme und Lösungswege. Berlin: Wissenschaftlicher Verlag.

Porter, A. (1960): Two British Symphonies. In: The Musical Times, Jg. 101, p. 766.

Poulton, Alan (1986): The Music of Malcolm Arnold, A Catalogue. London. Faber and Faber.

Prendergast, Roy (1992[2]): Film Music - A neglected Art. A Critical Study of Music in Films. London. Norton.

Redlich, Hans (1955): Reviews of new Music. In: The Music review, Cambridge. Volume 16, p.161-163.

Reschke, Renate Klio (2004): Chronos und Ästhetik. Zur historischen Dimension ästhetischen Denkens. In: Hirdina, Karin; Reschke, Renate (ed.) (2004): Ästhetik. Aufgabe(n) einer Wissenschaftsdisziplin. Freiburg. Rombach Verlag. Rombach Wissenschaften Reihe Litterae, p. 13–30.

Ridley, Aaron (2002): Aesthetics and Music. In: Baggini, Julian; Stangroom, Jeremy (ed.): New British Philosophy. The Interviews. London. Routledge, p. 59–74.

Riehn, Rainer (1998): Kot und Kunst. In: Metzger, H.-K.; Riehn, R. (ed.): Was heißt Fortschritt? München: edition text + kritik (Musik-Konzepte Band, 100), p. 68–70.

Rosen, Charles (1997 [1971]): The Classical Style. Haydn Mozart Beethoven. New York: Norton.

Saremba, Meinhard (1994): Elgar, Britten & Co. Eine Geschichte der britischen Musik in zwölf Portraits. Zürich/St. Gallen. M & T Verlag AG.

Schaarwächter, Jürgen (1994): Die britische Sinfonie 1914-1945. Köln. Verlag Dohr.

Schafer, Murray (1963): British Composers in Interviews. London: Faber and Faber.

Scherlies, Volker (1993): Zur Arbeitsweise Igor Strawinskys - dargestellt an der Symphonie d'instruments à vent. In: Danuser, Hermann; Katzenberger, Günter (ed.): Vom Einfall zum Kunstwerk. Der Kompositionsprozess in der Musik des 20. Jahrhunderts. Laaber: Laaber 4), p. 161–185.

Schneider, Norbert Jürgen (1997): Komponieren für Film und Fernsehen. ein Handbuch. Mainz. Schott (Reihe Studienbuch Musik).

Schönberg, Arnold (1984) [1946]: New Music, Outmoded Music, Style and Idea. In: Stein, Leonard (ed.): Style and Idea. Selected Writings of Arnold Schoenberg. Berkeley, California: University of California Press, p. 113–124.

Schuller, Gunther (1998): The compleat conductor. New York. Oxford Univ. Press.

Schüßler, Werner (ed.) (2000): Philosophische Anthropologie. Freiburg. Alber (Reihe Alber-Texte Philosophie, Teil 11).

Schwob, Rainer J. (2000): Klavierauszug und Klavierskizze bei Alban Berg. Untersuchungen zur Rolle des Klaviers als "Hilfsmittel". Anif/Salzburg. Mueller-Speiser (Reihe Wort und Musik, Teil 46).

Scowcroft, Philip L. (1997): British light music. A personal gallery of 20th-century composers. London. Thames.

Sloterdijk, Peter (1993): Weltfremdheit. Frankfurt. suhrkamp (Reihe Neue Folge Band, Teil 781).

Standop, Ewald; Meyer, Matthias L. G.; Standop-Meyer (2004): Die Form der wissenschaftlichen Arbeit. Ein unverzichtbarer Leitfaden für Studium und Beruf. Wiebelsheim. Quelle & Meyer (Reihe Arbeitshilfen).

Stasiak, Christopher (1987): The symphonies of Malcolm Arnold. In: Tempo, No 161/162 (June/September), Cambridge. University Press Cambridge. p. 85-90.

Stein, Leonard (ed.) (1984): Style and Idea. Selected Writings of Arnold Schoenberg. Berkeley, California: University of California Press.

Stephan, Rudolf (ed.) (1973): Zwischen Tradition und Fortschritt. Über das musikalische Geschichtsbewusstsein. Mainz. Schott (Reihe Veröffentlichungen des Instituts für neue Musik und Musikerziehung Darmstadt Band, Teil 13).

Tavaststjerna, Erik (2005): Jean Sibelius. Salzburg und Wien: Jung und Jung.

Trojahn, Manfred (1981): Formbegriff und Zeitgestalt in der "Neuen Einfachheit". Versuch einer Polemik. In: Kolleritsch, Otto (ed.): Zur "Neuen Einfachheit" in der Musik. Wien. Universal Edition. Studien zur Wertungsforschung Universität für Musik und darstellende Kunst, p. 83–89.

Troop, Richard (1999): György Ligeti. London. Phaidon Press Ltd.

Ünlü, Altug (2006): Gustav Mahlers Klangwelt. Studien zur Instrumentation. Frankfurt am Main. Peter Lang.

Walton, Chris (1994): Auf der Suche nach der Moderne in England. In: Kolleritsch, Otto (ed.): Klischee und Wirklichkeit in der Musikalischen Moderne. Wien: Universal Edition (Studien zur Wertungsforschung, 28), p. 256–271.

Walton, Susana (1980): William Walton. Behind the Facade. Oxford. Oxford University Press.

Whittall, Arnold (1997): Peter Maxwell Davies and the Problem of Classicizing Modernism. In: Danuser, Hermann (ed.): Die klassizistische Moderne in der Musik des 20. Jahrhunderts. Internationales Symposium der Paul Sacher Stiftung Basel 1996. Basel: Amadeus Verlag (Veröffentlichungen der Paul Sacher Stiftung Band, 5), p. 143–151.

___ (1999): Musical composition in the twentieth century. Oxford. Oxford University Press.

___ (2004): The later symphonies. In: Grimley, Daniel M. (ed.): The Cambridge Companion to Sibelius. Cambridge: Cambridge Univ. Press, p. 49–65.

Wiebe, Heather Luella (2005): Rituals of a lost Faith: Britten and the Culture of Post-War Reconstruction. Dissertation. Supervised by Taruskin, Bergeron und Vergon. Berkeley, California. University of California, Graduate Division University of California. Online at www.libumi.com/dissertations, UMI Number: 3187184,

Wintle, Christopher (ed.) (2005): Hans Keller. Essays on Music. Cambridge: Cambridge Univ. Press.

Wolterstorff, Nicholas (1980): Works and Worlds of Art. Oxford. Clarendon Press.

Young, Percy M. (1967): A History of British Music. London. Ernest Benn.